Contagious Adventist

Recognizing & Creating Faith Sharing Moments

PARTICIPANT'S EDITION

Foreword by Dwight K. Nelson

Marilyn Bauer
Dick Mackie
Esther R. Knott
Skip MacCarty

Contagious Adventist
Participant's Edition
Copyright © 2013
Pioneer Memorial Church
8655 University Blvd
Berrien Springs, Michigan 49103 USA
www.pmchurch.org
269-471-3133

Available from:
AdventSource
5120 Prescott Avenue
Lincoln NE 68506
1-800-328-0525
www.adventsource.org

Cover design by Robert Mason

The authors assume full responsibility for the accuracy of all quotations appearing in this text.

"Even now the reaper draws his wages, even now he harvests the crop for eternal life, so that the sower and the reaper may be glad together. Thus the saying 'One sows and another reaps' is true." John 4:36–37

"One scatters the seed; another gathers in the harvest; and both the sower and the reaper receive wages. They rejoice together in the reward of their labor." *Desire of Ages*, p. 192

Printed in the United States of America
ISBN 978-1-57756-782-0

"Therefore go and make disciples of all nations, baptizing them in the name of the Father and of the Son and of the Holy Spirit, and teaching them to obey everything I have commanded you. And surely I am with you always, to the very end of the age."

Matthew 28:19–20

Table of Contents

Foreword

I used to worry about the "impossibility" of reaching our world for Christ. Then I learned a lesson from Malcolm Gladwell's *The Tipping Point: How Little Things Can Make a Big Difference*. And now I don't worry anymore.

Gladwell takes the principles of epidemiology (the study of how diseases spread) and applies them to cultural trends. He shows that social change behaves much like a viral epidemic (such as AIDS, measles, or the common cold). All you need is a single virus with the ability to "stick" to someone else. And if the conditions are right, that single virus can literally infect an entire populace, creating an epidemic.

In fact, I once personally witnessed just such an "epidemic." It was at a pastoral staff meeting one afternoon at the Pioneer Memorial Church. Everyone was there, except our youth pastor, who walked in a half hour late with a runny nose, sneezes, and a pocketful of wet tissues. As he took his seat, I remember thinking, "I'm sure glad he's sitting between those two pastors and not by me!"

The next day I bumped into one of his seatmates. He looked miserable. "You got a cold?" He nodded wearily. "I bet I know where you caught it." He nodded again.

The following day I got a nasally phone call from the pastor who had been sitting on the other side. "Bet I know where you caught it," I intoned. "Me, too," she replied.

At home later that evening I was bragging about the great epidemiological discovery I'd made watching the transmission of a viral infection from one pastor to two others in a single setting. My wife Karen, a registered nurse, wasn't amused. "You shouldn't drive your pastors so hard," she countered. "Tell them that whenever they catch a cold, they need to take the day off and recover at home."

And so at our next staff meeting I passed along the counsel, being careful, of course, not to mention any names (particularly the youth pastor's). Then it came time for staff prayer fellowship, and none of us will forget how our youth pastor began his prayer: "O God, it is I, the infectious one..."

And that, writes Malcolm Gladwell, is how social epidemics get "effectively" started. All it takes is a single contagious viral agent—and in a matter of hours, an epidemic can be born.

What you hold in your hands is a prayerfully designed strategy that, through the power of the Holy Spirit, can transform you into just such a viral change agent for Christ—a cheerful, winsome, and contagious witness for your Savior. In a few short hours, you'll not only become infected by "the everlasting gospel"—the very good news that God has entrusted to our endtime community of faith. You'll also be equipped with a fresh, third-millennial strategy to share your faith *anywhere*—at work or at home, at school or at play, in the air or on the ground, over dinner or on the fly.

I personally know the team that produced this Contagious Adventist Seminar, field-tested it on this university campus before field-testing it on the road, and then created the accompanying video package. Every one of them is an effective and contagious change agent for Jesus and an active member or pastor of this congregation. For me they are the embodiment of Contagious Adventist Christians. And I'm honored to call them friends.

That's what Jesus calls you and me, too. "'You are My friends....You did not choose Me, but I chose you and appointed you that you should go and bear fruit'" (John 15:14, 16 NKJV). Given how close we now live to the edge of eternity and His return, isn't this the right time for you and me to pray the same prayer: "O God, it is I, the contagious one"?

Then by His grace and through His Spirit, let the epidemic begin!

Dwight K. Nelson
Pioneer Memorial Church

Acknowledgements

The writing team wishes to express appreciation to the many people who helped us develop and test this seminar.

- Pastor Dwight K. Nelson who commissioned this project.

- The small group (composed of brand new and lifelong Adventists and interested friends) who first tested the material: Larry and Janet Adams, Anne Carlson, Stephanie Elkins, David Fitzstephens, Josh and Nicole Price, Carrie Rhodes, Tim and Mary Nell Rosenboom, Holly Shaffer, Terry Vitek, and Khonnah Weithers.

- Those who graciously let us practice our earlier versions on them, allowing us to receive valuable feedback for the many revisions: 83 Michigan Conference Campmeeting seminar attendees, 67 Pioneer Memorial Church elders at the Elders' Retreat, SEEDS Conference seminar attendees, and NAD Church Ministries Conference attendees.

- Pioneer Memorial Church members and Andrews University students who attended the major test of the seminar in 2008 and the taping of the sessions in the Fall of 2009. Special thanks to Betty Guy for her technical support.

- Pastor Anthony WagenerSmith, Church Planter in the Florida conference who field-tested our leader's guide with his church planting team, and Pastor Jerry Chase of Akron, Ohio who along with his congregation field-tested our materials. Pastor Chad Stuart, Senior Pastor at the Visalia Seventh-day Adventist Church in the Central California Conference and Pastor Jerry Wasmer of the Florida Conference for the time they invested in critiquing and giving ideas for the leaders' guide.

- Merlin Burt, Director of the Center for Adventist Research at Andrews University and Katy Wolfer, special projects manager and research specialist, for their editing and fact checks in Session 9.

- Bryan von Dorpowski, who was the co-presenter during many of the test runs and is the co-presenter on the DVD. Thanks to Becky, Bryan's wife, who gave uncomplaining support to his participation.

- Carl Johnston at Seminars Unlimited for the services and expertise of Scott Grady and Stew Hardy in the areas of film production.

- Weimar College for the use of the acronym **NEWSTART** ® as a way to share health principles.

- Pioneer Memorial Church and the North American Division— Church Resource Center for their funding.

- Our families who put up with us being gone during the many evening, holiday, and Sunday working sessions: David Bauer, Ronald Knott, Olivia Knott, Lyn MacCarty, and Judy Mackie.

- We would like to acknowledge our appreciation to those who developed the *Becoming a Contagious Christian* course. We have conducted that seminar numerous times in our church and our members were so blessed by it that they asked us for a follow-up seminar designed specifically to share our Seventh-day Adventist beliefs.

Introduction

Welcome to the Contagious Adventist Seminar. The fact that you have opened this book and are reading it is the beginning of an answer to our prayers that God will raise up a generation of Seventh-day Adventists who will be equipped to share their faith in winsome and intentional ways. This participant's guide is designed to be used in connection with the Contagious Adventist Seminar. This is not a stand-alone book. However, we believe that once you have gone through the seminar, read the preview material, created your impact list, filled in the blanks, watched the videos, written your testimony, and explored the question-and-answer/response sections, you will want to keep this book nearby as a cherished reference.

There is one surprising thing we discovered along the way. Every time we have presented this seminar, participants have come to us and said, "It's amazing how God just keeps bringing people into my life for me to share with. This hasn't happened before. What's going on?" Through this seminar you will become more and more aware that God is bringing particular people across your path for the spiritual connection your relationship can give them. You may even have interacted with some of these people before, but just never recognized the spiritual potential of those contacts in the way that you will now. As you go through the seminar you will see with new eyes, you will listen in more intentional ways, you will be moved to act with more compassion, you will pray more, and you will open your mouth and share your testimony. So don't *you* be surprised when God fulfills His promise.

Here is how the nine 90-minute sessions are organized.

Sessions 1 and 9 are a bit unique, but beginning with Session 2, each session of the Contagious Adventist Seminar is organized into four sections:

1. **His Story.** Each session starts out with a short review of one of the major biblical beliefs of Seventh-day Adventists. These are the objective truths of the Bible as Jesus has given them to His people.

They are Jesus' story relative to that particular subject (the Great Controversy, the Sabbath, death, the Second Coming, etc.).

2. **Our Story.** This is the Testimony section in which we practice becoming consciously aware of how the biblical beliefs of Scripture have made a difference in our own lives. This is our testimony. If these beliefs have not impacted our lives in a positive way, then we have not integrated them yet ourselves. For most of us, they have become integrated, at least to some degree. In this section we become conscious of how these biblical beliefs have impacted us, making our lives better and deepening our love for God and others. Remember, according to Revelation 12:11, Satan is overcome by the combination of "the blood of the Lamb" (His story) and "the word of [our] testimony" (our story). When His story is combined with our story, it is a powerful witness God can bring to someone—through a contagious Adventist.

3. **Recognizing and Creating Contagious Adventist Moments.** In this section we learn and practice ways to interact with people. If we are good listeners, we will hear their story. Then the next step is to skillfully introduce Jesus' story to them in a way that intersects with their own story, being able at appropriate times and ways to share how our story has been impacted by His story. This has the potential to open their minds and hearts to Jesus and His story in ways they perhaps have never thought of, or perhaps even heard of, before.

4. **Decisions.** In this section, we learn how to ask questions appropriate to the occasion that will give people a chance to make Jesus' story part of their own story in a way that it is not presently. There is always an appropriate question that will move them along this path. In this section we look at some of those questions that can give our friends this opportunity. The goal of all witnessing is to help people discover the adventure and fulfillment that results from making Jesus' story part of their own story at levels they have not yet experienced.

You will get the most out of this seminar if you:

1. Pray daily that the Holy Spirit will work in your own life.

2. Pray daily for those on your "impact list."

3. Carefully read the preview material as you prepare to come to each session of the seminar.

4. During the session fully participate when you are asked to respond, write, and share.

5. Do the homework that is listed at the end of each session. When the principles become integrated into your life, then information leads to transformation.

6. Make yourself available to God each day.

We are already praying for you.

Please share your stories with us at: www.contagiousadventist.org.

Session 1

Why Become a Contagious Adventist?

In this session we will:

1. Understand the purpose of the Contagious Adventist Seminar.
2. Review points from the *Contagious Christian* course.
3. Affirm the message and mission of the Adventist Church.
4. Formulate and share our personal *Contagious Adventist* testimony.
5. Begin to develop our impact list.

A. Purpose of the Contagious Adventist Seminar

The purpose of the Contagious Adventist Seminar is to introduce our members to the art of being contagious Adventists.

The objective is for participants to learn the skills of converting routine, everyday experiences into spiritual conversations that will attract others in winsome and friendly ways and create in them a desire to learn more of what the Bible teaches about Jesus.

A key thought to remember:

God calls us to _____ others to what we believe,

not to _____ it on them.

What an extraordinary journey God invites us to share with Him.

Be wise in the way you act toward outsiders; make the most of every opportunity. Let your conversation be always full of grace, seasoned with salt, so that you may know how to answer everyone.
Colossians 4:5–6

The Contagious Adventist Seminar will:

1. Affirm the importance of the _____

    _____ and _____.

2. Create an awareness of evangelistic opportunities in

    _____ experiences.

3. Demonstrate how Contagious Adventism actually works.

4. Model how to _____ key Bible teachings.

5. Provide the opportunity for participants to develop and practice sharing their personal testimony in relation to the biblical teaching.

6. Define the steps for leading someone to a _____.

B. Three key points from the *Contagious Christian* course:

1. Links in a Chain:

["He who is a child of God should henceforth look upon himself as a link in the chain let down to save the world, one with Christ in His plan of mercy, going forth with Him to seek and save the lost." *Desire of Ages,* p. 417]

2. Different Styles of Evangelism:

You can be *yourself* and let God work through your personality and gifts.

"There are different kinds of gifts....All these are the work of one and the same Spirit, and he gives them to each one, just as he determines." 1 Corinthians 12:4, 11

3. Barbeque First:

["If we would humble ourselves before God, and be *kind and courteous and tenderhearted and pitiful* [empathetic], there would be one hundred conversions to the truth where now there is only one. *Testimonies,* vol. 9, p. 189, emphasis supplied]

C. Why Be a Contagious Adventist?

Some wonder why it is important for us to share with people who are already Christians the more complete understanding of the Bible truths entrusted to Adventists.

1. _____ God's command

   a. Jesus specifically instructed the church to be "teaching them to obey everything I have commanded you." Matthew 28:19–20

   b. Matthew 7:12 says, "So in everything, do to others what you would have them do to you, for this sums up the Law and the Prophets."

c. God desires everyone to have a *full* knowledge of the truth, and has sent the Holy Spirit to "guide you into *all* truth." (John 16:13, emphasis supplied)

2. _____ God's passion

3. _____ God's character

a. Isaiah 26:8 says: "Your name and renown [fame] are the desire of our hearts." In other words, "We are passionate about Your reputation, God."

b. "The last rays of merciful light, the last message of mercy to be given to the world, is a revelation of His character of love." *Christ's Object Lessons*, p. 415

4. _____ against deception

a. Satan's final deceptions will be so powerful that they will "deceive, if possible, even the elect." Matthew 24:24 NKJV

b. The apostle Paul warned the early church to be on guard against false teachers who would lead them away from truth. Acts 20:29–31

c. The Three Angels' Messages of Revelation 14

5. _____ the promise of a hope-filled life now

a. "I have come that they may have life, and that they may have it more abundantly." John 10:10 NKJV

b. "And you shall know the truth, and the truth shall make you free." John 8:32 NKJV

VIDEO: Why Become a Contagious Adventist?

a. What is your reaction to what you heard?

_____

_____

_____

b. What is the motivation to be a Contagious Adventist?

_____

_____

_____

D. Two Keys to Becoming a Contagious Adventist

Revelation 12:10–11 speaks of "the accuser of the brethren" finally being cast down. "And [the saints] overcame [Satan] by the _blood of the Lamb_ and by the _word of their testimony_, and they did not love their lives to the death." (NKJV, emphasis supplied)

According to this text, there are two keys to overcoming Satan's influence in our lives. In this seminar we will look at how we can use these same keys to help overcome Satan's influence in the lives of others.

- The blood of the Lamb—sharing _____ story.

- The word of their testimony—sharing _____ story.

1. The Blood of the Lamb: Sharing _His_ Story

a. We call this the _____ truth of the gospel—_His Story_—a story that stands as truth whether or not we accept it, or our lives are affected by it.

b. All the truths of the Bible find their center and meaning in the life, death, and resurrection of Jesus.

c. This is the objective truth of the gospel. This is _His_ story.

2. The Word of Their Testimony: Sharing _Your_ Story

This is the _____ truth of the gospel.

It is "_your_ story."

Your Contagious Adventist testimony is the story about the difference the gospel has made in your life. The gospel is not simply a set of cold, objective, sterile truths to be *acknowledged*. It is a power to be *experienced* in our lives. It is the point at which *information* leads to *transformation*.

E. Four Biblical Components of a Contagious Testimony:

1. _____ that God has done something great in your life.

   "The Mighty One *has done great things for me*—holy is His name." Luke 1:49 (emphasis supplied)

2. _____ those experiences in your heart.

   "Mary *treasured* up all these things and pondered them in her heart." Luke 2:19 (emphasis supplied)

3. _____ with others.

   "Return to your own house, and *tell* what great things God has done for you." Luke 8:39 (NKJV, emphasis supplied)

   "Our confession of His faithfulness is Heaven's chosen agency for revealing Christ to the world. We are to acknowledge His grace [the truths of the Bible] as made known through the holy men of old; but that which will be most effectual is the testimony of our own experience...these precious acknowledgments to the praise of the glory of His grace, when supported by a Christ-like life, have an irresistible power that works for the salvation of souls." Ellen White, *Ministry of Healing*, p. 100

4. _____ others to Jesus.

   "And many of the Samaritans of that city *believed in Him because of the word of the woman* who testified, 'He told me all that I ever did.' So when the Samaritans had come to Him, they urged Him to stay with them: and He stayed there two days. And many more believed because of His own word. Then they said to the woman, 'Now we *believe*, not because of what you said, for *we ourselves have heard Him* and we know that this is indeed the Christ, the Savior of the world.' " John 4:39–42 (NKJV, emphasis supplied)

God works through your testimony to reach the hearts of others, as well as to bind your heart to His.

Your testimony is developed when you:

- *recognize* the great things God has done for you and

- *treasure* those things in your heart.

Your testimony becomes contagious when you:

- *share* it with others and

- *lead* them to Jesus.

F. Developing Contagious Adventist Skills

What is *your* story?

Begin by thinking about your answer to the following question:

What *difference/influence* has the Seventh-day Adventist truth and life-style made in my life?

1. If you are a **convert to the church,** tell:

   a. What drew you to the Seventh-day Adventist Church

   b. What led you to become a member

   c. What difference the Adventist message and experience have made in your life.

2. If you **grew up as a Seventh-day Adventist,** tell how you are blessed by that spiritual heritage. Here are a few guidelines that will help:

   a. If you **cannot identify a specific time** of your conversion, simply tell the story briefly of how you were raised by Adventist parents and a church who taught you the love of God. You have been spared much of the pain and hardships of those who lived a life apart from God and had more dramatic conversions. Tell your praises.

b. If you had a ***defining moment***, perhaps a crisis (death, divorce, or financial struggle) or a joyful moment (birth of a child or grandchild), describe the specific experience or period of your life when God worked in very identifiable ways to draw you to conversion and the assurance of salvation.

3. If you were ***raised Adventist and subsequently left the church*** and later came back, that story is your testimony.

a. What did God do to draw you back?

b. What difference has it made in your life since you came back?

c. What difference has it made in the lives of those around you?

 VIDEO: Sharing your Adventist testimony

My Testimony

INSTRUCTIONS: In the space below, outline your testimony regarding the difference/influence the Seventh-day Adventist truth/lifestyle has made in your life. Use the above categories as a guide to writing your Contagious Adventist testimony.

_____

_____

_____

_____

_____

_____

_____

_____

_____

_____

_____

_____

_____

_____

_____

_____

_____

_____

_____

My Impact List

Name	Contact Information	Next Step
1. _____	_____	_____
	_____	_____
	_____	_____
2. _____	_____	_____
	_____	_____
	_____	_____
3. _____	_____	_____
	_____	_____
	_____	_____
4. _____	_____	_____
	_____	_____
	_____	_____
5. _____	_____	_____
	_____	_____
	_____	_____

a. Begin praying for the people on your list.

b. Remember that a prayer priority soon becomes a calendar priority.

c. Ask God to help you recognize the Contagious Adventist Moment.

d. Ask God to help you create the Contagious Adventist Moments.

e. Ask God to help you lead others to make a decision to join the movement of those who call others to the fuller truth about God.

f. See the appendix for nine ways to pray for those on your impact list (from *Praying Church Source Book*).

G. Homework

This seminar is more likely to bring about a life change if you practice what you have learned during the session and if you come to class prepared.

1. **Read preview material for Session 2.**

   The preview will introduce the foundational belief of Seventh-day Adventists: Jesus is Lord.

2. Continue to develop your impact list and pray that God will provide specific openings for you to connect with each one.

3. Ask one or two other Adventists why they think it is important to be a Seventh-day Adventist—what difference being an Adventist has made in their lives.

4. This week, share your testimony about the difference the Adventist truth has made in your life. You might share your story with another Adventist or with someone on your impact list. Be open to God's leading.

   One of our participants from an earlier seminar simply told her colleague at work that she was taking a class and that she had to share her story with someone for part of her homework. Of course the colleague wanted to help her out.

PREVIEW FOR SESSION 2: JESUS IS LORD

Jesus Is Lord

Each of us is a Christian because we accepted Jesus as Lord of our life. It is only through Jesus that our life has meaning. He is our Creator, our Redeemer, our dearest Friend, and our soon-coming King. He is the basis for our hope, the inspiration for our love, the promise of our faith.

Through Him and with Him all things are possible. Because of Jesus, we are no longer bound by sin. Because of Jesus, death has no claim upon us. Because of Jesus, we can be called the children of the Most High God and heirs to His eternal kingdom.

Contagious Adventists Because...Jesus Is Lord

We want to be Contagious Adventists not primarily because of any unique doctrine of our Church or because we think we are better than other people. We want to be Contagious Adventists because of what Jesus has done for us personally with the wonderful miracle He has performed in our lives—a miracle so marvelous, so life-giving, and so life-restoring that it cannot be denied or hidden. It must be shared.

We want to be Contagious Adventists because we want the whole world to have what we have. We want the world to have Jesus.

Common Ground

Just because Adventists hold in common with other Christians the belief that Jesus is Lord, we should not minimize its importance in our spiritual conversations. When talking to a Christian of another denomination, confessing our faith in Jesus as Lord establishes common ground. When talking to a non-Christian, confessing our faith in Jesus as Lord lays the only foundation upon which a genuine religious experience can be built.

Foundational Belief and Testimony

Jesus is Lord—that is our foundational doctrine. As a Church, Seventh-day Adventists believe that Jesus is who He claimed to be and is everything else the Bible claims Him to be. When this doctrine becomes part of our own experience and is shared with others as a personal testimony, it is a powerful instrument the Holy Spirit can use to effect salvation. (Revelation 12:11)

You—A Contagious Witness

There are no shortcuts to winning people to God and to the fuller truths of His Word. The adage: "People don't care how much you know until they know how much you care" applies here more than in any other aspect of life. This was one of Jesus' great secrets in winning people. He was constantly thinking of the good He could do for others. He treated them with genuine love and they sensed it and responded to it. Contagious Adventists show the same qualities. They are friendly and outgoing. They listen when people share their concerns. They assist others in need. They extend sympathy and love. This is a true investment in people. This is how you win their confidence.

Jesus never met anyone whom He did not see as a candidate for His eternal kingdom. There were no chance encounters with Jesus. He believed that each encounter served some higher purpose than merely the situation or need at hand. In the same manner, every time you have an encounter with someone, it represents a Contagious Adventist opportunity, a time to share Jesus.

Spiritual CPR

In the medical field all personnel are taught the skills of Cardio Pulmonary Resuscitation—CPR. This a life-saving procedure performed on people suffering specific medical emergencies. This procedure has saved many lives.

We invite you to think of your spiritual encounters with others (Cultivating, Planting, Reaping) as Spiritual CPR—CPR for eternal life. Every time you interact with a potential interest, you can contribute in some way toward one of these steps.

> The first stage of "**cultivating** the soil" is learning how to "prepare the way" as John the Baptist did for Christ. We do this by arousing the curiosity of seekers so they will want to hear the good news. That doesn't mean we blindly engage in stage one with every seeker we meet. We need to pay attention, for perhaps the curiosity of the seeker has already been aroused. If this is the case, then we may have the opportunity of sharing the gospel, which is the second stage, called "**planting** the seed." Yet even announcing the gospel is not enough. At the right time we need to sensitively point out that God desires a response or decision to be made. In other words, the third stage is "**reaping** the harvest," which involves an appeal to the will to make a commitment to Christ. Only God can make the human response positive. But evangelism isn't fully understood unless there is the hope to produce a harvest.
>
> *Out of the Salt Shaker & Into the World* by Rebecca Manley Pippert (pp. 138–139, emphasis supplied)

A Link in God's Chain

Remember, you are just one link in the chain. Pray for discernment to know where someone is in their spiritual journey. As the Spirit leads, give the invitation ever so carefully and simply to take the next step. This is the essence of being a Contagious Adventist.

If someone chooses not to accept the fuller truth you have shared, do not take it personally; it is not you they are rejecting. Jesus set the example to keep expressing genuine interest in people regardless of their response. And never stop praying for them. God can bring other influences, other links in His chain, into their lives to help them take the next step. With Jesus all things are possible.

Session 2

Jesus Is Lord: The Foundation for "Contagious Adventist"

In this session we will:

1. Identify four scriptural characteristics of a contagious witness for God.

2. Identify the first Bible teaching a Contagious Adventist should share.

3. Outline and share your testimony related to "Jesus is Lord."

4. Practice Contagious Adventist skills with a partner.

5. Learn how to ask questions.

6. Demonstrate how to recognize and create spiritual openings.

A. Scriptural Characteristics of Contagious Adventists

Four scriptural characteristics of a contagious witness for God:

1. A _____ relationship with God

To be effective witnesses for God, we must spend time daily talking to God and reading/contemplating His Word. (Matthew 4:4)

2. Complete _____ on the Holy Spirit

On our own we cannot win anyone to Jesus or to His church. Jesus said, "Apart from me you can do nothing." (John 15:5)

3. Show _____ _____ in people

"Christ's methods alone will give true success in reaching the people. The Savior mingled with men as one who desired their good. He showed His sympathy for them, ministered to their needs, and won their confidence. Then He bade them, 'Follow Me.'" *Ministry of Healing*, p. 143

4. Authenticity—be genuine, _____ _____!

a. It is important to be authentic in acknowledging that we are not immune from trials and temptations or spiritual struggles. Yet we have hope.

b. We should not try to portray that we have all the answers to life's mysteries and know all there is to know about Bible truth. Yet we can acknowledge that we are excited to share what we have learned.

c. A personal testimony has three parts:
Our struggle
Our hope
And the acknowledgment that we too are fellow seekers.
(No one likes a "know-it-all.")

ACTIVITY (1)

List some places we can go in order to make friends outside of our church circle.

_____

_____

_____

_____

_____

_____

_____

_____

_____

Not everyone we develop a witnessing relationship with will be open to the fuller truths we wish to share. But that is the responsibility of the Holy Spirit, not yours or mine.

Our responsibility is to:

1. Be prepared at all times to testify to the hope that we have (1 Peter 3:15).

2. Invite others to share in that hope.

3. Leave the results to the Holy Spirit.

ACTIVITY (2)

List some ways we can show genuine interest in people.

_____

_____

_____

_____

_____

_____

_____

_____

_____

_____

_____

_____

_____

B. Theme Statement: Jesus Is Lord—First Things First

1. Starting Place: Adventists' Foundational Teaching

The great message of the New Testament is that Jesus—the incarnated, crucified, resurrected, ascended, interceding, and returning Jesus—is Lord. Until people know that we _believe_ Jesus is Lord and _follow_ Him as Lord, our distinctive truths will be understood out of context.

It is always good to begin a conversation about your beliefs by establishing _common ground._

2. The Two-Part Affirmation that Jesus Is Lord

"They overcame him by the blood of the Lamb and by the word of their testimony..." Revelation 12:11

This affirmation to the Lordship of Jesus Christ has two parts:

the _____ _____ that Jesus is *Lord*

your _____ _____ that Jesus is *Lord* of your life.

a. The Biblical Teaching—His Story
Jesus is our _____
(Genesis 1:26–27; Romans 5:12; 6:23)

Jesus is our _____
(John 3:16; 1 Corinthians 15:2–4; 2 Corinthians 5:18–21)

Jesus is our _____ _____

(John 14:15, 21; 2 Corinthians 5:15–17; 1 Peter 1:3–9; 2:24)

Jesus is our _____
_____ (John 14:1–3)

b. The Personal Testimony—*Your Story*
Below are some examples of testimonies that illustrate how to share that "Jesus is Lord" of your life:

1. William
I've found Jesus to be a wonderful Savior. He empowers my life. He's my Lord and my treasured Friend.

Many people confuse being "religious" with being a "Christian." Let me explain. Being "religious" usually means people focus on what they DO—a list of rules and regulations. But being a "Christian" focuses, first, on what has already been DONE in the life, death and resurrection of Jesus Christ. Not only have I allowed Him to be my Savior. I have asked Him to be the Lord of my life. This has brought me a sense of purpose and hope that I wouldn't trade for anything.

I have some rules that I live by, but not so I can be religious. What Jesus has done affects everything I do. I live as I do because the Bible tells me that it's the way I can bring the greatest glory to God. And that's the great goal and joy of my life.

All of my beliefs as a Seventh-day Adventist are based on the Bible and are windows through which I can perceive the nature of the spiritual conflict that is raging both in the world and in my own heart. Through these beliefs I can also see and better understand a more beautiful and complete picture of God.

2. Helen

I understand and believe that Jesus died for my sins. That is the basis for my salvation. Because He gave His life for me, I can trust Him with my life. I've asked Him to be the Lord of my life, and that decision affects everything I do.

3. Richard

I've chosen to make Jesus the Lord of my life because of all He has done for me. That decision affects everything I do. And I'm learning every day what it really means to let Him be Lord of my life.

4. John

As a five-year-old, I accepted Jesus Christ as my Savior. At fourteen, I committed myself to Christ as Lord. And now, having entered my fifties, I still confess those initial commitments. But I have come to a greater understanding of the richness of God's love in Jesus Christ. The testimony I could trumpet simplistically as a teenager, I now declare with a tear in my voice. In my youthful idealism, I half-believed that I really deserved God's grace and perhaps could have earned it, that I was even doing him some kind of favor to receive it. Now I am painfully aware that in spite of being created in God's image, I have self-destructive tendencies that daily cause me to depend upon the Lord's initiative on my behalf. I realize that my hope really is based on nothing less than Jesus' blood and righteousness. Now I have committed all I know and don't know of myself to all I know and don't know of God in Jesus Christ.

John Huffman, Jr., *NIV Couples Devotional Bible* (Grand Rapids, MI: Zondervan, 1994), p. 1301 on Philippians 1:6.

ACTIVITY (3)

Outline your brief testimony that "Jesus is Lord." NOTE: This has a different slant than what you outlined in Session 1.

_____

_____

_____

_____

_____

_____

_____

_____

_____

_____

_____

_____

ACTIVITY (4): Questions about your beliefs

What are some questions people have asked you about your beliefs or your church?

_____

_____

_____

_____

_____

_____

_____

_____

_____

_____

When someone asks you about your distinctive beliefs, the following are some possible ways to **begin** your answer.

(Remember this is only the **first part** of the answer.)

1. Every religion has its distinctive beliefs and so do Seventh-day Adventists. However, our foundational belief—that Jesus is Lord—is shared by many other Christian churches....

2. Thanks for asking. The basis of my belief has to do with Jesus—what He has done for me personally and what He has done for all of us....

3. I'd love to tell you what my church believes about Jesus, and what Jesus means to me.

 VIDEO

ACTIVITY (5): Practice skills with a partner

From the list of questions we just created on the previous page, choose one of the questions that people have asked you about your beliefs or your church. Practice a response that bridges into a statement/testimony that Jesus is Lord. (Include your brief testimony that "Jesus is Lord.")

Once you have shared the biblical teaching and/or your testimony that Jesus is Lord, *then* **give a brief, direct answer to the question initially raised** and perhaps explain how that particular belief helps you better understand the goodness of God's character. Then you may want to say something like the following:

"Can you see that when Jesus is Lord it would affect...

... when I worship?"

... how I spend my money?"

... what I eat?"

Make the question appropriate to what was initially asked.

It may then be appropriate to make a decision-type invitation.

(Possible responses to some of the questions raised in **ACTIVITY (4)** will be provided in later sessions.)

C. Asking for a Decision

1. Guidelines for asking for decisions:*

a. Use a series of questions to determine the level of decision a person is ready to make.

b. Always begin with general questions to determine their understanding of the subject and if they need further information. If more information is needed, make arrangements to provide it before proceeding to the next level.

c. Proceed from one level of questions to another as long as you continue to get a positive response. When you do not get a positive response, you can say something like, "Thanks for sharing your thoughts on this. I'll keep you in my thoughts and prayers."

d. Based on their responses to the questions you have asked, prayerfully determine an appropriate "next step" for them. No matter how they answer the questions you ask, there is always some appropriate "next step."

e. After you ask a question, wait for an answer. Do not be afraid of silence. Silence creates a vacuum. If you do not break it the other person will. They will likely answer your question directly or indirectly.

f. It may be that the person does not have an answer at that time, but the very fact that they have heard the question is like a seed being planted. They will think about it. God will bring it to their mind at the appropriate times.

*Material in this course about decisions has been influenced by Mark Finley's *Decisions: Persuading People for Christ* (General Conference of Seventh-day Adventists Ministerial/Stewardship Association, 1984).

2. Progressive Levels of Questions:

The following grid suggests three progressively escalating levels of questions. These questions would be appropriate to ask after you have shared the Bible truth and your own personal testimony that "Jesus is Lord." When multiple options are provided, they will be indicated by numbers. (They are not progressive.) Pray that the Holy Spirit will guide you in determining the most appropriate option, which may be different than those suggested.

	Question(s) for a Christian	Question(s) for a Non-Christian
Level 1: Understanding Grasp of "Jesus is Lord" truth (includes biblical truth and your personal testimony related to it)	1. "I can tell by our conversation that you are a Christian." [Wait for them to respond.] 2. "What are your thoughts about how I understand the role Jesus wants to have in our lives? Does it make sense to you?"	1. "Does what I have shared, about Jesus as Lord, make sense to you?" 2. "What are your thoughts about this?"
Level 2: Desire Sense of personal need for the benefit that following Jesus as Lord could add to their life	"I often long for a deeper experience with Jesus. Do you feel that way yourself?"	1. "How would you feel about having that kind of experience yourself?" 2. "How would your life be different if there was someone who would always accept you and love you, no matter how much you messed up?" 3. "Do you ever wish you had something that would give you hope beyond this life?"

	Question(s) for a Christian	Question(s) for a Non-Christian
Level 3: Conviction How strongly they feel it is important to have Jesus be the Lord of their life	1. "When you face hard choices in life, do you find yourself asking, 'What would Jesus want me to do?'" 2. "Sometimes I struggle to have regular time with God. When I do spend regular time with Him, I am so blessed. I'd love to hear how you've struggled and been able to work this out."	1. "At this stage in your life, if someone were to ask you if you would like to have Jesus as the Lord of your life, how would you answer them?" 2. "Have you ever thought about asking Jesus to be Lord of your life?"
Next Step: Appropriate follow-up action they, or you, might take in support of their spiritual journey, based on your perception of their readiness to accept it	1. "Would you like to pray together right now?" 2. "Would you be interested in reading a book [*Desire of Ages*] on the life of Jesus?"	1. "Would you be interested in studying the Bible with me? 2. "Would you be interested in reading a book [*Desire of Ages*] on the life of Jesus?" 3. "I will be remembering you in my thoughts and prayers."

Remember, regardless of what the immediate results appear to be, the Holy Spirit will always use such conversations to reach hearts for eternity.

3. Texts Related to "Jesus is Lord"

Asking for a decision can be most effective when it is coupled with God's Word.

The Bible—
  has creative power,
  brings conviction,
  converts the soul, and
  generates spiritual life.

a. "If you love me, you will obey what I command." John 14:15

b. "Whoever has my commands and obeys them, he is the one who loves me. He who loves me will be loved by my Father, and I too will love him and show myself to him." John 14:21

c. "Yet to all who received him, to those who believed in his name, he gave the right to become children of God." John 1:12

d. "For God so loved the world that he gave his one and only Son, that whoever believes in him shall not perish but have eternal life." John 3:16

e. "Believe in the Lord Jesus, and you will be saved—you and your household." Acts 16:31

D. Contagious Adventist Skills

1. Recognizing and creating spiritual openings

   a. Helping in a personal crisis.

   _____

   _____

   b. Welcoming a visitor at church.

   _____

   _____

   c. Seizing a conversational opportunity.

   Someone may make a comment, or you may observe them doing something which you could turn into a **C**ontagious **A**dventist **M**oment (CAM). By arousing their curiosity you are cultivating the soil and maybe even planting a seed.

   Look for ways to find common ground by affirming what you see God is already doing in their lives.

   Consider these comments and possible CAM responses:

   1) You see someone coming home from church on Sunday.

      CA response: _So few people go to church anymore. It's nice to see that you've given God an important place in your life. What was one of the best things at your worship service today? (Tell me about the sermon you heard today.)_

   2) You see someone playing with a child or raising their kids well...

      CA response: _When I see the love you give your daughter, it reminds me of God's love for me. Your child is going to grow up with wonderful pictures of God because of your love._

3) Someone opens a door or helps you.

CA response: *You sure are a Good Samaritan.*

4) Someone shares something significant that they accomplished that day.

CA response: *It sounds like God really used you to accomplish something very important today.*

5) Someone is helping out with the youth group at their Sunday Church.

CA response: *You've taken on a big job. Kids really need adults who will care for them. I sure do admire you. I'll be praying for your ministry.*

6) Someone says, "I'll light a candle for you." (In some religions, the members often light a candle to a saint representing a prayer, on someone's behalf.)

CA response: *Thank you. It's great to know that you believe in prayer. I need more friends who will pray for me.*

7) You observe that someone is working hard to make their life better.

CA response: *I can see that you are responding to the movement of the Holy Spirit in your life.*

8) Someone says, "I wish I didn't get angry and swear so much."

CA response: *The good news is that at least now you feel bad about it. I'd say that means you're letting God work in your life.*

d. Learning the art of asking questions.

There is also an art to asking questions specifically designed to arouse curiosity and generate interest—*cultivating the soil.*

Possible questions or actions might be:

1. I'd love to hear the story of how you became a Christian. Will you share it with me?

2. You attend church regularly. How do you think we could get more people to know about God's love for them?

3. You seem to choose a really healthy lifestyle. Does it have anything to do with your spiritual beliefs?

4. Another thing you may do to generate interest is to say a blessing for a meal, whether it be in your home, cafeteria, restaurant, or lunch room. Pray out loud for your meal with friends and remember to thank God for your friend(s) by name.

Remember: "At that time you will be given what to say, for it will not be you speaking, but the Spirit of your Father speaking through you." (Matthew 10:19–20)

E. Homework:

1. **Read preview material for Session 3**—the unifying theme of Scripture.

   Do NOT wait until the last minute to read the assignment. Read it early as there is an assignment you need to spend some time thinking about.

2. Ask God to help you be aware of the openings He is creating. Come prepared to share an experience with the class at the next session.

3. Continue to develop your impact list and pray for how God would have you connect with each one.

4. This week, say "hello" to at least five people you do not know.

5. Show genuine interest to someone new or someone on your impact list.

PREVIEW FOR SESSION 3:
THE GREAT CONTROVERSY STORY

Preparing for an Assignment

During Session 3 you will be asked to think of some way that the Great Controversy story has blessed you or perhaps added hope to you at some specific time in your life. Pray about this and think it through before you come to class.

Act 1: Before the Creation of the World

Before anything in the universe was brought into existence, God existed. The Bible says that God's entire character is summed up in love. This means that every act of God is rooted in love. All of God's creation, animate and inanimate, was designed for the free expression of love.

God's plan was an environment where everyone loved each other, where every impulse brought love, joy, and peace. That is how God meant life should always be—in heaven and on earth (Job 38:4–7; Psalm 90:2; Matthew 7:9–12; 1 John 4:8).

Act 2: War in Heaven

The peace of the cosmos was shattered with all the shock of a September 11 event. The Bible says, "war broke out in heaven." Lucifer, a perfect angel, rebelled and led a campaign against God's character and motives.

Lucifer the "morning star" became Satan the "accuser." Satan claimed that God's laws for governing the universe were maliciously intended and dictatorially imposed, with the purpose of limiting the freedom and happiness of His created beings. He accused God of selfishly restricting the angels' freedom to prevent them from gaining powers similar to His own.

Satan maligned God's character and through deception won the loyalty of one third of the heavenly angels. Ultimately those in rebellion were banished from heaven. God didn't destroy the disloyal band lest the loyal angels come to serve Him from fear of punishment. God seeks only the voluntary allegiance of love and trust. (Deuteronomy 30:15–16; Joshua 24:14–15; Isaiah 14:12–14; Ezekiel 28:14–15; John 8:44; Revelation 12:7–10)

Act 3: Paradise Created

At some time after the banishment of Satan, Planet Earth was created. Scripture says this earth was a gorgeous paradise, teeming with many species of life. The crowning act was the creation of man and woman in the very image of God Himself. Adam and Eve were created with the full power of choice. God placed one restriction on them: the "tree of knowledge of good and evil" that was in the midst of the garden. God forbade Adam and Eve to go near the tree or eat of its fruit.

The forbidden tree symbolized two things for Adam and Eve:

1) They were authentically free to say "no" as well as "yes" to God's commands.

2) Their life and happiness would be sustained for all eternity only as they lived in a loving, obedient relationship with God. (Genesis 1; 2:15–17; Titus 1:1–2)

Act 4: Paradise Lost

It is no surprise that the one place God warned Adam and Eve to stay away from was the one place God allowed Satan access to them.

One day Eve wandered away from Adam and found herself at the forbidden tree. Satan appeared in the form of a serpent and accused God of selfish motives in withholding the fruit from this tree. "Trust me, not God" was his message.

Tragically, Eve chose to believe Satan. First she and then Adam ate the forbidden fruit. When they sinned, Satan gained a base of wickedness on this earth—paradise was lost and the Great Controversy spread to this earth. Today the battle rages between good and evil—on our planet and in our hearts. Satan brings personal tragedy, natural calamities, and wars in an effort to hurt God by hurting those God loves. And we have no power of our own to find our way back to God and paradise lost. (Genesis 3:1–7; Romans 3:10–19; 5:12; 8:20–22; 1 Peter 5:8)

Act 5: The Promise

A plan for rescuing humanity from Satan's power was established by God and His Son before the "foundation of the world was laid." After Adam and Eve's sin, it was time to reveal this plan—the plan of salvation.

God visited with Adam and Eve in the cool of the evening. In essence they blamed each other, the serpent, and God Himself for their sin. God sadly announced that the natural consequence of their sin was hardships, the frailties of old age, and ultimately death. But He also spoke words of great hope to them. He promised that the power of the adversary, the serpent, would be broken by the seed of the woman. As the promise was more fully unfolded, it revealed how God would defeat the adversary through the woman's Seed—He would send His own eternal Son, who would suffer the assaults of Satan, take sins of Adam and his descendants upon Himself, and die in their place. Thus He provided them with an opportunity to gain the original plan—eternal life. It was to be each person's choice to accept or reject the gift of eternal life through Jesus Christ our Lord. (Genesis 3:15; Isaiah 53; Habakkuk 2:4; Luke 21:16–19; Romans 8:28; 16:20; Titus 1:1–2)

Act 6: Jesus, the Promised Savior

God Himself came to earth in the person of Jesus—the promised Messiah. Born in the Bethlehem stable, He was "Immanuel—God with us." Throughout His earth-life, Jesus was subjected to the full brunt of Satan's attacks. "In all our affliction, He was afflicted."

Through His life of loving service, Jesus revealed the character of God as it had never been shown before. *Through His death* for our sins, He showed Satan's accusations about God to be total lies. And *through His resurrection* from the grave, Satan's ultimate scourge of death was defeated. God was the Victor! (Isaiah 63:9; Matthew 1:23; 7:12; John 3:16; 13:34; 1 Peter 2:9, 24–25)

Act 7: Paradise Restored—The Grand Finale

One day Jesus will return to this earth. He will come to take with Him to heaven all who through faith and loving obedience have accepted God's gift of salvation. God will make a final end of sin, of death and sorrow, making a new heaven and new earth. God will be our God and we will be His people. We will be introduced to eternal life in the earth made new—Paradise Restored.

Throughout eternity we will never get tired of telling of God's faithfulness and love in rescuing us from a world of sin to life eternal in the paradise recreated. The Great Controversy will be ended—forever. (Isaiah 11:6–7; John 14:1–3; Ephesians 2:6–7; Revelation 21:3–5)

NOTE: During Session 3 you will be asked to think of some way that the Great Controversy story has blessed you, added hope to you perhaps, at some specific time in your life. Pray about this and think it through before you come to the next session.

We are living in the time between Paradise Lost and Paradise Restored and so we see the force of this war in the world around us and feel it in our personal lives. The Bible and the history of the Christian church present in sweeping detail this Great Controversy that has been raging from the time that Paradise was lost until that time when Paradise will be restored. God always has a people through whom He is trying to advance the cause of truth, letting others know about the plan He has so they can be saved. Satan does not want the story to be told. All through Scripture we see how God chose a people to share His message and how Satan attacked them. After the Cross, God raised up the Christian church to carry His side of the Great Controversy. Satan attacked the Church, and succeeded in bringing in false teachings that destroyed the truth and defamed God's character. God once again has raised up a movement that will reveal the truth about His character to a world that so desperately needs the hope He can give. We are part of that movement. Scripture makes it clear that Satan will once again attack God's people. But the war will soon be over.

Session 3

The Great Controversy: The Unifying Theme of Scripture

In this session we will:

1. Present a synopsis of the Great Controversy story you read in the Preview for this session.

2. Illustrate the Great Controversy story with a diagram.

3. Outline and share your testimony related to the Great Controversy.

4. Learn the skills needed to use the Great Controversy story as a Contagious Adventist.

5. Practice Contagious Adventist skills with a partner.

6. Learn how to ask for decisions related to the Great Controversy.

The Unifying Theme of Scripture

The Great Controversy story is the unifying theme of the Bible, under which all other truths can be grouped and integrated into a coherent whole.

A. **The seven short paragraphs:**

1. **Before the Creation of the World**—The Bible says that before anything else existed in the universe, God and the angels lived in peace, harmony, and love in heaven.

2. **War in Heaven**—At some time in the immeasurable past, Lucifer, one of God's perfect angels, abused the freedom God gave him. He rebelled against God and there was war in heaven. This rebel angel, Satan, and the angels who followed him, were cast out of heaven.

3. **Paradise Created**—Genesis records God's creation of our earth and all its life forms in a perfect state of paradise. Humanity was created in God's own image, fully capable of living in perfect obedience to God's law. Harmony reigned on earth as it once did in heaven.

4. **Paradise Lost**—Satan had access to this earth and succeeded in tempting Adam and Eve to disobey God. Suffering and death soon followed. Sin and alienation from God resulted for all human beings.

5. **The Promise**—God intervened on our behalf with the promise to send His own eternal Son, the Savior, to reconcile us to God. Through faith and obedience, we would again have the hope of eternal life in paradise restored.

6. **The Savior**—Jesus Christ was born into our world to reveal the character of God as it had never been seen before. Through His life of service and love He experienced trials and suffering just as we do. He died for our sins so that all who believe in Him might live forever.

7. **Paradise Restored**—Jesus promised to come again for those who accepted and followed Him. They will be with Him in heaven and then on this earth when paradise is restored.

B. **This sentence** will help you draw the simple diagram that is at the bottom of the page.

Before the Creation of the World, War in Heaven caused **Paradise Created** to become **Paradise Lost**; but God gave **The Promise** that the **Savior** would bring **Paradise Restored.**

C. **The diagram:**

The Great Controversy
The Unifying Theme of Scripture

Before the Creation of the world	Paradise Created	The Promise	Paradise Restored
	War in Heaven	Paradise Lost	The Savior

Activity (1): Writing the Sentence and Drawing the Diagram

Write the sentence here:

_____

_____

_____

_____

Draw the diagram here:

D. Personal Testimonies

1. Dick

When I heard this story, Satan became real to me. The church I used to belong to never talked about the devil. I thought he was just a figment of people's imagination. Now I know I have a real spiritual enemy and that my life is a spiritual battle. It helped me recognize my need for God more than ever.

2. Steve

I grew up in a Seventh-day Adventist home and heard the Great Controversy story from childhood up. But it really took on a deeper meaning when I went through a divorce. That was a very hard experience. I realized then just how much power Satan has to mess up our lives. I held fast to God's promise (Romans 8:28) that He will bring good out of every circumstance if we keep trusting Him. I couldn't do it on my own, but I kept praying for it. Looking back now I see many ways that God cared for me through that experience and I love Him now more than ever before.

3. Mary

The final act of the Great Controversy story always gets me. The thought of Jesus' return and being with Him eternally puts my daily problems into perspective. It gives me hope. On bad days I think to myself: "The Bible says we won't have it easy in this life. But the day is coming that will make it worth it all." That thought gives me the lift I need.

4. Marilyn

Why does God allow bad things to happen to good people? My 25-year-old son, our only child, was killed in a plane crash. Satan could not have done anything to bring us more pain. Although Satan meant that the tragedy should destroy our faith, God turned it to something that strengthened our faith, and helped us reach many young adults for His kingdom. God is truly the Victor in the Great Controversy.

Activity (2): Individual Exercise

Write your brief story of how the Great Controversy has influenced your life.

_____

_____

_____

_____

_____

_____

_____

_____

_____

_____

_____

_____

_____

_____

_____

_____

_____

_____

_____

_____

E. Developing Contagious Adventist Skills

Recognizing/creating openings

When you discuss the Great Controversy with someone, you do not necessarily have to tell the entire story. Just emphasize the part of the story that pertains to their particular situation or interest at the time.

The following are examples of opportunities to recognize and create the Contagious Adventist Moment so you will have the opportunity to share the biblical teaching of the Great Controversy story.

1. S_____

2. C_____ events

   a. God allows suffering in a sinful world but promises not to allow more than we can handle with Him (1 Corinthians 10:13). It is also true that God is able to bring some good out of all circumstances (Romans 8:28).

   b. Scripture shows that violence and loss of natural affection are signs of the last-day struggles between good and evil (Romans 1:31 KJV; 2 Timothy 3:3 NKJV).

   c. Satan knows that his time is short and he is seeking whomever he can destroy (Revelation 12:12).

   d. I read something that brought me a lot of comfort. It is from a book that was written more than 100 years ago: "God never leads His children otherwise than they would choose to be led, if they could see the end from the beginning, and discern the glory of the purpose which they are fulfilling as coworkers with Him." *Desire of Ages*, pp. 224–225

3. C_____

4. M_____ subjects

Here are some follow-up responses depending on the movie:

a. Crime, violence, broken relationships:

It's interesting the Bible talks a lot about that.
Would you like to know how we got into such a mess?
Would you like to know the real story behind that?

b. We all like a happy ending/feel good movie:

I know of one story where people really do end up living "happily-ever-after."
Have you heard the story about the Prince who saved a whole planet?

c. Star Wars type movies:

It seems Hollywood gets its themes right out of the book of Revelation. There's a story like that in the Bible.

Have you ever heard the Bible's Star Wars story?

5. Q_____

VIDEO

ACTIVITY (3) Share the Great Controversy story with a partner integrating your testimony.

F. Asking for a Decision

1. Guidelines for asking for decisions:

a. Use a series of questions to determine the level of decision a person is ready to make.

b. Always begin with general questions to determine their understanding of the subject and if they need further information.

If more is needed, provide that information, or make arrangements to provide it, before proceeding to the next level.

c. Proceed from one level of questions to another as long as you continue to get a positive response. When you do not get a positive response, you can say something like, "Thanks for sharing your thoughts on this. I'll keep you in my thoughts and prayers."

d. Based on their responses to the questions you have asked, prayerfully determine an appropriate "next step" for them. No matter how they answer the questions you ask, there is always some appropriate "next step."

e. After you ask a question, wait for an answer. Do not be afraid of silence. Silence creates a vacuum. If you do not break it the other person will. They will likely answer your question directly or indirectly.

f. It may be that the person does not have an answer at that time, but the very fact that they have heard the question is like a seed being planted. They will think about it. God will bring it to their mind at the appropriate times.

2. Progressive Levels of Questions:

After you have presented the Bible truth and your own testimony regarding the Great Controversy theme, the following grid of progressively escalating questions will help you determine the level of decision a person is ready to make. When multiple options are provided, they will be indicated by numbers. (They are not progressive.) Pray that the Holy Spirit will guide you in determining the most appropriate option, which may be different than those suggested. And remember, regardless of what the immediate results appear to be, the Holy Spirit will always use such conversations to His advantage to reach hearts for eternity. Trust in God and He will ensure that your faithful efforts bear fruit.

	Question(s) for a Christian	Question(s) for a Non-Christian
Level 1: Understanding Grasp of the Great Controversy theme (includes the biblical truth and your personal testimony related to it)	1. "Is this story as I've shared it pretty much how you understand the events and issues involved in the spiritual warfare?" 2. "Do you have questions about how I understand the issues involved in the spiritual warfare?"	1. "Does the story I've shared about the spiritual war taking place between God and the evil one make sense to you?" 2. "Do you have questions about any of this?"
Level 2: Desire Sense of personal need for the benefit that the Great Controversy theme could add to their life	1. "The trouble is, often it seems that I falter in this struggle. As the apostle Paul said, 'When I want to do good, evil is right there with me.'" 2. "I want to represent Jesus constantly in my life. I find I need to daily return to God's Word for help to be able to do that. What is your experience like?"	1. "The struggle between good and evil is real in my own life. Do you ever struggle between good and evil?" If they answer "Yes," then ask them, "Do you know for sure which side of that battle you are on?" If they answer "Yes" say, "Your recognition of this struggle is evidence that you have already been responding to God's plan for you whether you are aware of it or not. God wants you to be with Him for eternity. Would you like that?"

	Question(s) for a Christian	Question(s) for a Non-Christian
Level 3: Conviction How strongly they feel it is important to choose their allegiance in the Great Controversy	1. "I have found that when I go to the Scriptures I sometimes discover something that challenges my beliefs; but when I work through them, I come to a deeper and more beautiful understanding of God and His plan for me. 2. "Have you found things that have challenged your beliefs and understanding of God?" If they answer yes, then ask, "How have you worked through such challenges?"	1. "Is there anything to prevent you from making a conscious choice to be on God's side?" 2. Assuming they are ready to make a choice, you could ask them, "Would you like to receive Jesus as your Savior now?" If they would, you could help them pray the prayer of acceptance you learned in the *Contagious Christian* course. If they say they are not ready to make such a choice, you could say, "I hope you'll think about it. I will be remembering you in my thoughts and prayers."
Next Step Appropriate follow-up action they, or you, might take in support of their spiritual journey, based on your perception of their readiness to accept it	1. "Would you be interested in reading a book on this subject?" (For example: *Patriarchs and Prophets, Desire of Ages, Great Controversy, Steps to Christ,* or *Christ's Object Lessons.*) "I would be happy to send/give/loan it to you." 2. Would you like to pray together right now?"	1. "Would you be interested in studying the Bible with me?" 2. "Would you be interested in reading a book on this subject?" (For example: *Patriarchs and Prophets, Desire of Ages, Great Controversy, Steps to Christ,* or *Christ's Object Lessons.*)

You can call the Adventist Book Center's toll-free number (1-800-765-6955) or log on to their website (www.adventistbookcenter.com) and be connected to the ABC nearest you, or talk with your pastor, and get advice as to what book they would recommend for the subject your friend is interested in.

3. Texts Related to "The Great Controversy"

a. "As he went along, he saw a man blind from birth. His disciples asked him, 'Rabbi, who sinned, this man or his parents, that he was born blind?' Neither this man nor his parents sinned,' Jesus said, 'but this happened so that the work of God might be displayed in his life.'" John 9:1–3

b. "For our struggle is not against flesh and blood, but against the rulers, against the authorities, against the powers of this dark world and against the spiritual forces of evil in the heavenly realms." Ephesians 6:12

c. "And we know that in all things God works for the good of those who love him, who have been called according to his purpose." Romans 8:28

d. "No temptation has seized you except what is common to man. And God is faithful; he will not let you be tempted beyond what you can bear. But when you are tempted, he will also provide a way out so that you can stand up under it." 1 Corinthians 10:13

e. "Since the children have flesh and blood, he too shared in their humanity so that by his death he might destroy him who holds the power of death—that is, the devil—and free those who all their lives were held in slavery by their fear of death." Hebrews 2:14–15

f. "Submit yourselves, then, to God. Resist the devil, and he will flee from you." James 4:7

Session Wrap-Up

Whatever questions you are asked impinge on this Controversy.

Whatever answer you give should reveal the true character of God, refute the deceptions of Satan, and reaffirm that Jesus is Lord.

Pray, believing that God will help you know how to respond.

G. Homework

1. **Read the preview for Session 4**—God's gift of time.

2. Practice the Great Controversy story diagram with someone this week—a co-worker, family member, or church friend.

PREVIEW FOR SESSION 4: THE SABBATH

In previous sessions we learned that Jesus is Lord but Satan contests Jesus' Lordship and attempts to destroy the bond we have with our Creator. God was well aware of the danger Satan posed for His new Creation, so He wove into the fabric of Creation a sacred time, sanctified and set apart, holy unto the Lord (Genesis 2:1–3) in which God's children could receive a special blessing each week and renew their bond with their Creator. This special time was the Sabbath.

Each day during Creation week God saw what He had created and declared it good, but only the seventh day was blessed and set apart as holy. The six days of Creation would supply all our material needs, but our spiritual relationship with our Creator was represented by the Sabbath. After sin entered our world through Adam, the Sabbath manifested protective benefits and was imbedded by God in the heart of His moral constitution for all humanity—the Ten Commandments (Exodus 20:8–11; Deuteronomy 5:12–15; Mark 2:27–28).

Sabbath Blessings

Among the numerous blessings God intended the Sabbath to provide are the following:

1. **Purpose:** The Sabbath reminds us that we do not exist by accident. We were created by a loving God who made us in His image and desired a personal and intimate relationship with us— our ultimate purpose (Exodus 20:8–11; 31:17; Ezekiel 20:12).

2. **Redemption:** The Sabbath reminds us of God's commitment to deliver us from the bondage and penalty of sin, and to restore us to holiness so that we might live a life that blesses others and brings glory to God, and ultimately be with Him forever (Exodus 31:12; Deuteronomy 5:12–15; Ezekiel 20:20).

3. **Assurance:** The Sabbath symbolizes God's invitation for us to rest in Him and in the finished work of Christ for us. Our own works are faulty at best, so the basis for our security in this life and our assurance of heaven is our relationship with Him (Hebrews 4:4–9).

4. **Restoration**: The Sabbath provides us with needed time for nurturing and restoring our most important relationships—with God, family, and friends—and for serving one another (Matthew 12:11–13; Mark 2:27–28).

5. **Health**: The Sabbath provides us, and those we live with and employ, with divinely mandated, energy-restoring, health-promoting rest from our regular work schedules (Exodus 20:9–10).

On Sabbath we cease our frantic pace and our over-committed lifestyles, and we rest that the Lord might replenish us, that our strength, our joy, and our faith might be renewed. Then we may go forth into the new week rejoicing—assured of the Lord's presence in our lives and rededicated to the Lord's service (Isaiah 58:13–14).

It is little wonder that believers throughout biblical history observed the seventh-day Sabbath, or that the redeemed will observe the Sabbath throughout eternity as a perpetual symbol and celebration of their redemption through Christ. The chart below shows the continuity of the Sabbath from Creation to the New Earth.

God/Adam and Eve	Israel	Ten Commandments	Jesus
Genesis 2:1–3	Exodus 16	Exodus 20:8–11	Luke 4:16

Apostles	Gentiles	Eternity
Acts 16:13	Isaiah 56:1–8 Acts 13:44	Isaiah 66:22–23

The Role of the Sabbath in the Great Controversy

Because of its great blessing potential for the benefit of humanity, God's holy Sabbath has been pinpointed in the crosshairs of the deceptive and destructive purposes of the great archenemy of God and human beings. Satan tries to deceive people into believing that any day of rest and any form of worship is sufficient. This transforms the Sabbath into a mere concept or principle. The Sabbath is neither. The Sabbath is a sacred moment in time. It holds a special blessing that can be received only within that framework of sacred time.

Daniel prophesied that a religious power would arise that would "try to change the set times and the laws" that God Himself had ordained for humanity's benefit including the Sabbath (Daniel 7:25). It happened exactly as prophesied.

In the early Christian centuries the leaders of the church, without any scriptural support, pulled away from the seventh-day Sabbath and advocated Sunday sacredness in an effort to protect the church from being identified with the Jews who worshipped on the seventh day and were despised throughout the Roman Empire.

During the Dark Ages church leaders hoarded in monasteries the few copies of the Scriptures that were available. They forbade their members from possessing any portion of the Bible and did not allow it to be translated into the languages spoken by the people. Because of this, people did not have the opportunity to compare the practice of Sunday worship with the specific instruction of the fourth commandment to remember the seventh day as the Sabbath.

Through the centuries, however, there were always some groups of people who risked their lives to preserve the Scriptures and who did observe the seventh-day Sabbath. Seventh-day Adventists are inheritors of that rich spiritual heritage.

The book of Revelation commissions God's people with "the eternal gospel to proclaim to those who live on the earth—to every nation, tribe, language and people..." saying, "'...Worship him who made the heavens, the earth, the sea and the springs of water,'" language borrowed directly from the fourth commandment and, by implication, tying the proclamation of the gospel to the proclamation of the seventh-day Sabbath (Revelation 14:6–7).

Within that same context, Revelation warns people against receiving "the mark of the beast" which is set in contrast to the experience of God's people "who obey God's commandments and hold to the testimony of Jesus" (Revelation 12:17). The final confrontation in the Great Controversy between God and Satan will center on worship and include God's holy Sabbath as a watershed issue. The last great battle to be fought on this earth will not be a political or military conflict fought in the Middle East, but a spiritual conflict in the hearts of people all over the world. The victors will be those who "obey God's commandments and remain faithful to Jesus" (Revelation 14:12).

Session 4

The Sabbath: God's Gift of Time

In this session we will:

1. Discuss the limitation of time in our lives and the stress that it causes.

2. Understand that the Sabbath is God's gift of time—a sacred time of rest, renewal, and communion between God and His creation.

3. Understand how the Sabbath points to God as both Creator and Redeemer.

4. Outline and share your testimony related to the Sabbath.

5. Practice Contagious Adventist skills with a partner.

6. Learn appropriate responses to questions about the Sabbath.

7. Learn how to ask for decisions related to the Sabbath.

The Sabbath

A. Spiritual background of the people you may encounter.

1. _____ background—

Do _____ respect the authority of Scripture.

2. _____ background—

Who believe in the continuing _____ of the Ten Commandments.

3. _____ background—

Who do _____ believe in the continuing validity of the Ten Commandments.

B. Brief Presentation of the Sabbath

1. The best way to spell love is ___ ___ ___ ___.

2. The seventh-day Sabbath was blessed and sanctified

_____ sin and became even more important

_____ sin.

We live in a spiritual "_____ zone."

The seventh-day Sabbath is a "_____ zone."

3. The seventh-day Sabbath is God's established sign that:

a. God is our _____. (Exodus 20:8–11; 31:17)

b. God is our _____.
(Exodus 31:12–13; Deuteronomy 5:12–15; Ezekiel 20:12)

c. God is our _____.
(Exodus 16; Matthew 6:28–33; Hebrews 4:9–10)

d. God's last-day people "obey God's _____

and remain faithful to _____." (Revelation 14:12)

e. As Contagious Adventists we must be very clear regarding the critical importance of the Sabbath. *All questions on the Sabbath are ultimately questions about the sovereignty of God and our allegiance to Him.* These are questions intimately intertwined within the Great Controversy and should be answered from that perspective. Our responses should always affirm that Jesus is Lord. Jesus, Lord of our life, declared Himself Lord of the Sabbath (Matthew 12:8; Mark 2:28). As a sign of our allegiance and our desire for intimate fellowship with Him, we uphold, honor, and seek the blessings of His seventh-day Sabbath.

C. Personal Testimonies

1. Bonnie

My husband, Jim, a former Seventh-day Adventist, was in the hospital following an auto accident. Dave, a member of the church he used to attend, came to visit him in the hospital.

When Jim came back home, Dave came by the house to visit him again. During his visit I said to Dave: "My husband told me that he used to go to church on Saturday. If I may be so bold to ask, Why do you go to church on that day? It just seems a little strange to me."

I was a bit taken back when Dave said, "Thank you for asking. It's because Jesus is my Lord and I love Him."

I replied, "Jesus is my Lord, and I love Him too, but I don't go to church on Saturday."

Dave asked me for my Bible and read two texts to me. The first one was the fourth commandment that specifically mentioned the seventh day of the week as the Sabbath of the Lord. The second was John 14:21 NKJV, "He who has My commandments and keeps them, it is he who loves Me." Then Dave took me over to my calendar which was hanging on my wall in the kitchen, and asked me which day was the seventh day. Sure enough, it was Saturday. I began keeping the Sabbath from that day forward, and was eventually baptized into the Seventh-day Adventist Church.

2. **Carrie**

I grew up in the Adventist church and went to Sabbath School and church for all of my early years. When I got to college my life took a turn in a different direction. I wasn't professing any religion when I got married. It wasn't that I didn't believe in God, I just didn't go to church anymore. I didn't really miss it until I had my first child. Then I began to get a strange homesickness and I wanted my daughter to have what I had in my early years. Now that I'm back, I really appreciate the Sabbath. It isn't always easy because my husband isn't with me in this, but I pray that he will be someday. I try to make the Sabbath a very special day for my daughter.

3. **Winston**

I was fortunate to grow up in a home that observed the seventh-day Sabbath as a very special time. God said we are to make the Sabbath a delight, and my parents did that for us kids. Friday night was a special time with a favorite meal and stories. After church on Sabbath we often had friends over for lunch. Sometimes we joined church members in the afternoon for some outreach program for people in need, or to share the gospel. I will never forget those great memories. Those times helped bond us as a family. They helped keep God real for me. I want to provide the same special experiences for my children.

ACTIVITY (1)

Share your answer to the following question:

What blessings have you personally received from observing the Sabbath?

ACTIVITY (2)

Group presentation

D. Developing Contagious Adventist Skills

1. Starting conversations

a. If someone you're talking to expresses concern with the problems their children have to deal with in their neighborhood or at school, tell them that your children are involved in a great program that helps them deal with those same kinds of challenges. Then invite them to join you sometime when you and your children go to Sabbath School.

b. If you're having a special event at your church some Sabbath, invite a friend or neighbor to attend. During that event the question of why you go to church on Saturday is likely to come up. Share enough to wet their appetite (e.g., "It's the day God's asked us to keep in His commandments and it's been such a blessing to our family"). Then offer to give a more complete explanation from the Bible at another time soon. Then be sure to follow it up.

c. If you have a friend who's active in another church, you might at the appropriate moment say, "I have such respect for you and your commitment to Jesus. But I'm puzzled about something. Would you be willing to explain to me why you go to church on Sunday instead of on the seventh day of the week as the Bible teaches?"

d. When someone asks you what makes your church different, first affirm that Jesus is your Lord and Savior, and then share that you worship Him on the seventh day of the week as the Bible teaches.

e. If the question of the Sabbath has come up in a conversation you have had with someone, invite them to your home to watch a DVD/video about the Sabbath.

2. Challenging Texts:

a. Question: [Romans 14:5–6]

Doesn't Romans 14:5–6 say that the important thing is that you are convinced in your own mind about what day you should worship on, not the actual day itself, and that if you believe there's no special day at all for worship, then that's the truth for you?

Possible Response:
In Romans 14:1 Paul says he is discussing "disputable matters." The seventh-day Sabbath God gave in the Ten Commandments was never a "disputable matter." The "special days" Paul was referring to in Romans 14:5–6 were the ceremonial feast days and ceremonial holy days, such as the Passover, etc. The question was, "Is it wrong for a Christian, perhaps one with a Jewish background, to still observe the Passover, for instance?" Paul's answer was that in such "disputable matters," let each decide for themselves.

b. Question: [Colossians 2:13–15] (see Q/A—Objections/Responses)

But I thought Colossians 2:13–15 says that the Ten Commandments were nailed to the cross when Jesus died and thus don't apply to us anymore.

Possible Response:
These verses are not talking about the Ten Commandments. What it actually says is, "He [Christ] forgave us all our sins, having canceled the written code, with its regulations, that was against us and that stood opposed to us; he took it away, nailing it to the cross." Which of the Ten Commandments would be considered against us or opposed to us?
[For more on this, see Appendix A, Session 4, Q5]

c. Question: [Colossians 2:16]

Doesn't Colossians 2:16 say that we should not let anyone judge us as to whether we worship on a Sabbath or not?

Possible Response:

The sabbaths referred to in Colossians 2:16 are qualified in verse 17 as those that "are a shadow of the things that were to come; the reality, however, is found in Christ."

There were two kinds of Sabbaths in the Bible. The first kind was the seventh-day weekly Sabbath instituted by God in Eden before sin.

The other kind of sabbath was the ceremonial sabbaths connected to the annual feasts that were associated with the Old Testament sanctuary ceremonial system.

The commentary note of the New International Study Bible on this text says: "The ceremonial laws of the OT are here referred to as the shadows (cf. Heb. 8:5; 10:1) because they symbolically depicted the coming of Christ; so any insistence on the observance of such ceremonies is a failure to recognize that their fulfillment has already taken place."

Expanded responses to these three texts are found in Appendix A, Session 4.

E. Asking for a Decision

1. Guidelines for asking for decisions:

a. Use a series of questions to determine the level of decision a person is ready to make.

b. Always begin with general questions to determine their understanding of the subject and if they need further information. If more is needed, make arrangements to provide it before proceeding to the next level.

c. Proceed from one level of questions to another as long as you continue to get a positive response. When you do not get a positive response, you can say something like, "Thanks for sharing your thoughts on this. I'll keep you in my thoughts and prayers."

d. Based on their responses to the questions you have asked, prayerfully determine an appropriate "next step" for them. No matter how they answer the questions you ask, there is always some appropriate "next step."

e. After you ask a question, wait for an answer. Do not be afraid of silence. Silence creates a vacuum. If you do not break it the other person will. They will likely answer your question directly or indirectly.

f. It may be that the person does not have an answer at that time, but the very fact that they have heard the question is like a seed being planted. They will think about it. God will bring it to their mind at the appropriate times.

2. **Progressive Levels of Questions:**

After you have presented the Bible truth and your own testimony regarding the Sabbath truth, the following list of progressively escalating questions will help you determine the level of decision a person is ready to make. When multiple options are provided, they will be indicated by numbers. (They are not progressive.) Pray that the Holy Spirit will guide you in determining the most appropriate option, which may be different than those suggested. And remember, regardless of what the immediate results appear to be, the Holy Spirit will always use such conversations to His advantage to reach hearts for eternity. Trust in God and He will ensure that your faithful efforts bear fruit.

	Question(s) for a Christian	Question(s) for a Non-Christian
Level 1: Understanding Grasp of the Sabbath truth (includes the biblical truth and your personal testimony related to it)	1. "Does what I've been presenting about the Sabbath make sense to you?" 2. "Do you have questions about what the Bible teaches about the Sabbath?"	1. "Does what I've been presenting about the Sabbath make sense to you?" 2. "Do you have questions about why I consider the Sabbath so important?"

	Question(s) for a Christian	Question(s) for a Non-Christian
Level 2: Desire Sense of personal need for the benefit that the Sabbath truth could add to their life	"I know that you are committed to following God and His Word faithfully. How have you personally worked through the issues raised by God's command to observe the seventh-day Sabbath?"	"Can you see how God's gift of the seventh-day Sabbath each week exclusively for the purpose of focusing on the ultimate purpose of life, spending time with family and friends, and having time for relating to others in need could be a real blessing?"
Level 3: Conviction How strongly they feel it is important to act on Sabbath truth	"What would keep you from observing the seventh-day Sabbath of the fourth commandment?"	"Would you be interested in joining my family some Sabbath afternoon and experiencing for yourself the blessing that the Sabbath is to us?"
Next Step Appropriate follow-up action they, or you, might take in support of their spiritual journey, based on your perception of their readiness to accept it	1. "Would you be interested in attending church with me on a Sabbath sometime soon?" 2. "I'll be praying that you will soon be experiencing the blessing of Sabbath observance for yourself." 3. "Would you be interested in reading a book about the Sabbath?" 4. "Would you be interested in coming over to my place some evening to have some refreshments and watch a very interesting video about this subject?"	"Would you like to come over to our house some evening for some refreshments and to watch a really good video on this subject?"

3. Decision Texts Related to the Sabbath

a. "By the seventh day God had finished the work he had been doing; so on the seventh day he rested from all his work. And God blessed the seventh day and made it holy, because on it he rested from all the work of creating that he had done." Genesis 2:2–3

b. "Remember the Sabbath day by keeping it holy. Six days you shall labor and do all your work, but the seventh day is a Sabbath to the LORD your God. On it you shall not do any work, neither you, nor your son or daughter, nor your manservant or maidservant, nor your animals, nor the alien within your gates. For in six days the LORD made the heavens and the earth, the sea, and all that is in them, but he rested on the seventh day. Therefore the LORD blessed the Sabbath day and made it holy." Exodus 20:8–11

c. "'As the new heavens and the new earth that I make will endure before me,' declares the LORD, 'so will your name and descendants endure. From one New Moon to another and from one Sabbath to another, all mankind will come and bow down before me,' says the LORD." Isaiah 66:22–23

d. "Then he said to them, 'The Sabbath was made for man, not man for the Sabbath. So the Son of Man is Lord even of the Sabbath.'" Mark 2:27–28

e. "If you love me, you will obey what I command." John 14:15

f. "This calls for patient endurance on the part of the saints who obey God's commandments and remain faithful to Jesus." Revelation 14:12

 VIDEO

F. Homework

1. **Read the preview for Session 5** which unmasks one of Satan's great deceptions.

2. This week look for opportunities to arouse curiosity by inserting comments about the blessings of the Sabbath.

PREVIEW FOR SESSION 5: DEATH AND BEYOND

"You will not surely die" (Genesis 3:1–4).[1] This was the original lie spoken by Satan in the Garden of Eden. Satan scoffed at God's warning to Adam and Eve that if they ate the forbidden fruit they would die. Thus began the erroneous teaching of the immortality of the soul. Through the ages Satan has succeeded in embedding this pernicious lie into the heart of the world's major religions, including many mainstream Christian denominations. The common misbelief is that upon bodily death the soul or spirit, which they believe is immortal, goes directly to heaven or hell or into some equivalent state of continuing consciousness. Near-death experiences seem to lend credence to such beliefs. Some people claim that during the brief period when they were clinically "dead" they went through a tunnel of light and met their own loved ones and/or a great being of light and love. However, it is clear that no one recorded in the Bible as being resurrected ever made such a claim (e.g., 1 Kings 17:17–24; 2 Kings 4:18–37; 13:20–21; Luke 7:11–15; 8:51–56; John 11:38–48; Acts 20:9–12).

The doctrine of the immortality of the soul has given rise to:

- A growing fascination with psychics, spiritualism, and the occult. Some people rely on supposed communication with dead relatives, friends, or other authority figures to guide them in making decisions.

- The veneration of saints and virtual deification of Mary as humanity's living, compassionate intercessor before God.

- Variations on the doctrine of purgatory which offers people the hope of a second chance to get right with God after they die.

- The doctrine of eternal torment in hell which maligns the character of God.

---

1. All quotations from the Bible in this preview are taken from the New King James Version.

Masterful Deception Unmasked

The Bible, however, closes the door tightly against this masterful deception. Of the 1,700 references to "soul" and "spirit" in the Bible, not one refers to either of them as immortal or undying. The Bible states emphatically: "The soul that sins shall die" (Ezekiel 18:4), and God "alone has immortality" (1 Timothy 6:14–16).

Formula for Human Creation

At creation, God formed Adam out of the "dust" of the ground and breathed into him the "breath" or "spirit" of life (Genesis 2:7). The formula established here is as follows:

Dust of the ground + Breath of life from God = Living soul/person who comes into being.

The Hebrew word for "breath" in Genesis 2:7 is *ruach*, which is the same word used in Ezekiel 37:5–14 which the NIV text note says may be translated as "breath," "wind," or "spirit" and in fact is translated as such interchangeably throughout these verses. The Greek word used in the New Testament for "breath," "wind," or "spirit" is *pneuma*. The last thing dying people do is *breathe out* their last *breath* (literally "expire" [ex-*spirit*], "*breathe* out") which the Bible describes as their *spirit* (Hebrew, *ruach*; Greek, *pneuma*) returning to God (Ecclesiastes 12:7).

Formula for Human Death

The Bible thus depicts death as the reverse process of creation in the following formula:

Body returns to dust – breath/spirit returns to God = Person ceases to exist.

The life-and-death cycle can be likened to making a box and taking it apart again. The formula for making the box would be:

Boards + Nails = Box.

When you remove the nails from the boards and disassemble the box, where does the box go? Nowhere! It simply ceases to exist. Death is like that.

What Happens When You Die?

Note how clearly the Bible depicts the state of death as a deep, unconscious, dreamless sleep:

- Jesus likened death to an unconscious sleep. Death is called sleep over 70 times in the Bible. (John 11:11–14)

- "The dead know nothing," and all their emotions have vanished. (Ecclesiastes 9:5–6)

- The dead cannot remember God or praise Him, which they certainly would do if they were in heaven with God. (Psalm 6:5; 115:17)

- Even king David, one of the Bible's giants of faith, is not in heaven, but is asleep in the grave. (Acts 2:29, 34)

- Paul, in the only funeral sermon recorded in the Bible, does not try to console grieving Christians with the assurance that their faithful loved ones are in heaven with God enjoying a happy life. Rather, he offers the consolation that they are asleep until the day of resurrection at the Second Coming of Jesus when God will wake them and call them forth to be with Him forever. (1 Thessalonians 4:13–18)

The Bible specifies two types of death. The first death occurs at the end of a person's life on this earth. In the first death you will not go directly to heaven or hell or anywhere else. You will simply go to sleep until the resurrection at Jesus' Second Coming (John 5:28–29; 1 Corinthians 15:51–53). The Bible also speaks of a second death which the unsaved will experience after the judgment. The second death is an eternal death, as the Bible describes it: "they shall be as though they had never been" (Obadiah 15–16).

The Power Behind the Psychics

Psychics who offer to communicate with your deceased loved ones cannot do so, for your loved ones are in a deep, unconscious sleep and know nothing between the time they die and the day of resurrection. The intimate information psychics appear to receive from "departed spirits" is received instead from satanic spirits who have access to the most intimate details of our lives. For this reason, it is dangerous and forbidden by God to even attempt to communicate with the dead (Deuteronomy 18:10–13).

No Fear of Death for Those Who Trust in and Follow Jesus

Death was not part of God's original plan. Had Adam and Eve obeyed God, they would have lived forever (Titus 1:2). Sin brought death (Romans 5:12). But just as "the wages of sin is death," even so "the gift of God is eternal life in Christ Jesus our Lord" (Romans 6:23). Union with the Life-Giver equals life; separation from the Life-Giver results in death. "He who has the Son has life; he who does not have the Son of God does not have life" (1 John 5:12).

Session 5

Death and Beyond: Unmasking Satan's Deceptions

In this session we will:

1. Review the biblical teaching of death and beyond.

2. Discuss some challenging texts.

3. Outline and share your testimony related to this teaching.

4. Practice Contagious Adventist skills with a partner.

5. Learn the skills needed to use this truth as a Contagious Adventist.

6. Learn how to ask for a decision related to death and beyond.

A. Death and Beyond

1. At creation God "set _____ in the hearts of men" (Ecclesiastes 3:11).

   Death inevitably raises profound questions such as:

   • What happens to a person when they die?

   • Can the living communicate with the dead?

   • Where do psychics get their information?

   • Is there life after death?

   Such questions provide one of the most natural bridges into discussions about what the Bible says about death, and they create a natural opening for you to share your testimony about the hope you have.

2. Most religions of the world teach some form of _____ of the soul.

3. Many people who reject the Bible truth on the state of the dead do so more for _____ reasons than for biblical ones.

   It is very important that when we talk about this subject the emotional issues are also addressed. Below are some points that can be emphasized in addressing the emotional issues involved:

   a. Our deceased loved ones rest in the grave as if sleeping peacefully in the arms of Jesus awaiting His call on resurrection morning.

   b. If our deceased loved ones were in heaven with God, then they could see what is going on down here: the suffering in the world, the trials of their friends and relatives, and the new relationships/marriages being formed.

   c. Perhaps one of the reasons God mercifully allows the dead to sleep until He returns is to shield them from the enormous pain and suffering that is so prevalent in the world. God alone bears that global weight.

4. Jesus rose from the dead and assures us that all who put
   their trust in Him and follow Him as Lord of their life will be
   _____ at His Second Coming.
   (1 Corinthians 15:3–4, 51–54)

B. Three Challenging Texts

1. Thief on the cross. Luke 23:43

When Jesus was crucified, He assured the repentant thief with
the following words: "'I tell you the truth, today you will be with
me in paradise.'" Many people will respond to this text by saying,
"Doesn't this clearly teach that when the thief died he went
directly to be with Jesus in heaven?

The following are key points to use to answer this question/
objection:

a. The Bible identifies Paradise as the place where God dwells
   (Revelation 2:7; 22:1–2). When Jesus was resurrected on
   Sunday morning (two days after He had died), He told Mary
   that He had **not yet** ascended to His Father (in Paradise)
   (John 20:17). Therefore, when Jesus told the dying thief on
   that Friday that "today you will be with me in Paradise," Jesus
   could not have meant that the thief would literally be with Him
   that very day in Paradise! (He had not gone there yet Himself.)

b. So, then what *did* Jesus mean by His statement to the thief?
   Since the original Greek text did not have punctuation marks,
   it is possible that the pause in Jesus' sentence should come
   after "today"—i.e., "Assuredly I say to you today, you will be
   with Me in Paradise." In this light, Jesus' statement gave the
   thief an immediate assurance ("this-day") that he would have
   eternal life (at the resurrection).

c. Here is a modern-day example of the difference that the
   position of a comma can make in the meaning of a sentence.

What does this sentence mean?

Woman without her man is nothing.

Place some commas/punctuation below to clarify the meaning of this sentence **for you.**

1) Woman without her man is nothing.

2) Woman without her man is nothing.

2. Parable of the Rich Man and Lazarus. Luke 16:19–31

Many take this story literally to mean that you go directly to heaven or hell when you die without waiting for any resurrection at the end of the world. This was a popular idea at the time of Jesus. So He took the idea, creating a story in order to make a point.

As you respond to this question/objection, keep the following key points in mind:

a. Jesus never intended His story of the rich man and Lazarus to be taken literally regarding the state of a human being in death. We can know this because the story is inconsistent with everything else Jesus taught in the Bible on this subject. Here are some of the contradictions with other biblical passages:

Literal story:	Heaven would be a place with mourning, crying, and pain because the saved could forever witness the suffering of lost loved ones and not be able to alleviate it.
Bible truth:	The Bible says that in heaven God "will wipe every tear from their eyes. There will be no more death or mourning or crying or pain." (Revelation 21:4)
Literal story:	When people die they are really still consciously alive.

Bible truth:	The Bible teaches that death is a state of unconscious sleep until the resurrection. (Ecclesiastes 9:5–6)
Literal story:	People go directly to heaven or hell when they die.
Bible truth:	In the resurrection the dead will come forth from their graves, not from heaven or hell. (John 5:28–29)

b. Jesus explicitly states His reason for telling the story. Verse 31 concludes by saying, "'If they do not listen to Moses and the Prophets, they will not be convinced even if someone rises from the dead'" (Luke 16:31).

The Jewish leaders often suggested that they would accept Jesus as the Messiah if He would produce some miraculous sign. To expose the fallacy of their claim, Jesus told this story, assigning the name "Lazarus" to the poor beggar whom the story says died and went to "Abraham's bosom" (Luke 16:20–23 NKJV). Then Jesus subsequently raised a man named Lazarus—the only person He raised from the dead for whom the Scriptures record a name (John 11). In doing so, Jesus did not say He was bringing Lazarus down from heaven, but waking him up from sleeping (John 11:11).

And did the Jews then believe in Jesus because He raised Lazarus from the dead? Hardly so. Rather, "From that day on they plotted to take [Jesus'] life," and "made plans to kill Lazarus as well, for on account of him many of the Jews were going over to Jesus and putting their faith in him" (John 11:53; 12:10–11). Which proved the very point Jesus was making in His story—If unbelievers will not be convinced of truth by the clear teaching of God's word in Scripture, neither will they be convinced by a miraculous sign from God (Luke 16:31). This is the great lesson of Jesus' story of the rich man and Lazarus, not that when someone dies they go directly to heaven or hell.

c. At this point, ask the person you are conversing with if they would be interested in studying what the Bible actually teaches about hell. (For a short study on hell, refer to question 3.)

3. Everlasting Fires of Hell. Matthew 25:41, 46; Revelation 14:11

Matthew 25:41, 46 says that on the final Day of Judgment Jesus will tell the lost to "Depart from me, you who are cursed, into the eternal fire prepared for the devil and his angels...then they will go away into eternal punishment." And Revelation 14:11 says "the smoke of their torment ascends forever and ever." That sounds like those who are lost in hell fire will not be asleep but will be consciously experiencing "eternal punishment."

Question One: Doesn't this contradict the belief that death is a sleep?

Possible Response Components:

a. The confusion comes, in part, from the failure to recognize the fact that the Bible specifies two types of death:

The first death:

1) A temporary death

2) which is an unconscious sleep

3) and leads to a later resurrection at the Second Coming of Christ (John 5:28–29; 11:11–14)

The second death:

1) An eternal death

2) which comes after the judgment

3) applies only to those who have rejected God

4) and leads to total annihilation and an end to one's existence. The Bible describes this second death as "they shall be as though they had never been." (Obadiah 15–16 NKJV)

	1st Death	2nd Death
1.	Temporary	Eternal
2.	Experienced by the righteous and the wicked	Experienced only by the wicked
3.	Unconscious sleep	An end to one's existence
4.	Leads to a later resurrection	Leads to total annihilation (at the end of the millennium)

Question Two: How can this be when the torment is to be "eternal"?

Possible Response Components:

The word "eternal" in the Bible can refer to either process or result. For example, the Bible says that the Old Testament cities of Sodom and Gomorrah that were destroyed by fire "serve as an example of those who suffer the punishment of eternal fire" at the end of the world (Jude 7; cf. Genesis 19; 2 Peter 2:6). In this text the term "eternal fire" refers to the result of the fire, not to the process. Sodom and Gomorrah are not still burning—the process has ended, but the result of the fire was eternal—those cities were completely destroyed and never rebuilt. In a similar way, Revelation 14:11's description of the fate of the unsaved as "the smoke of their torment ascends forever and ever" was language borrowed almost verbatim from Isaiah 34:9–10's description of the fate of the Old Testament city of Edom which was destroyed by enemies and never rebuilt. The Bible refers to the total destruction of Sodom, Gomorrah, and Edom as examples of what the "eternal fire" of hell will be like. It will not burn forever (process), but the destruction it accomplishes will last forever (result).

The Bible says that when Satan reaps the ultimate punishment for what he has sown, he will not burn forever, but *"shall be no more forever"* (Ezekiel 28:18–19). In other words, the fire of hell will result in Satan ceasing to exist forever. The Bible uses that same language to describe the ultimate and natural consequence of people refusing God and His offer of salvation. It says "they *shall be as though they had never been,"* in other words, eternal annihilation (Obadiah 15–16 NKJV). This is the "eternal punishment" Jesus spoke about in Matthew 25:26, 30.

This just makes sense, doesn't it? How could a God of love burn someone, torture them, for eternity? He would have to work a miracle to keep them alive in order for them to suffer longer.

Sinners who have refused God's offer of salvation would not be happy living with God in heaven. Therefore, by ending their existence, God would be acting both mercifully and justly. God will reluctantly accept the unrepentant sinner's choice, and as a loving parent God will grieve over every one of His lost children. Therefore, God passionately appeals to everyone today to turn to Him and trust in Him that they might not be lost (Ezekiel 33:11).

C. PERSONAL TESTIMONIES

1. Pat

When my teenage brother Peter died in an accident, the thought that he was in heaven with God brought me comfort. I often imagined him looking down watching out for me. One day my friend Eileen told me that people don't go to heaven when they die. I thought it was cruel to say my brother was still in the ground. The very thought was repulsive to me. I wondered why anyone would want to take away a belief that brought so much consolation to so many.

Finally I got up my courage and asked Eileen about her comment. She apologized for not realizing how her words affected me. She showed me Bible texts that clearly said that people who die are asleep until the resurrection at the end of the world. She explained how this protected Peter from seeing all the suffering in the world—even my own troubles. That idea helped me understand that the Bible teaching about the dead was not a harsh doctrine. If death had to be, God had allowed it in the best possible way.

2. Sheila

From early childhood I was exposed to the truths of the Bible. My parents read it to me at home and I learned more about it in Sabbath School and church school. I have always believed the Bible teaching about death being a sleep until the resurrection.

Believing this Bible truth has shielded me from many dangers. Being a curious person, I probably would have experimented with séances and the occult had I not known this truth. And when a very dear aunt died, I am sure I would have tried to contact her, not realizing I was doing something God had strictly forbidden. I'm very grateful for the protection this truth has given me.

3. Sherrie

I was always very close to my grandmother so her death was very hard on me. When I came out of her funeral I saw a violet tulip lying on the pavement. Tulips were grandma's favorite flower and violet was her favorite color. I took that as a sign that she was alive somewhere and would still be with me. I took a lot of comfort from that thought.

I married a man whose parents were Seventh-day Adventists. One day the subject of death came up and I learned that they believe death is only a sleep until the resurrection. I said I could never believe that. I told them about the violet tulip and what that had meant to me over the years.

They were very patient with me, but over a period of time they showed me what the Bible said about death. They suggested that God may have allowed the tulip to be there to give me assurance that my grandmother was safely sleeping, waiting for Him to wake her so we could be together again. That was a new thought—a beautiful thought. I've been a Seventh-day Adventist now for five years. I think the Bible's teaching about death being a sleep is a beautiful truth.

4. Teresa

When I was a little girl my daddy usually tucked me into bed. But sometimes he would just hold me and rock me to sleep in his favorite chair. That was the most secure feeling I can remember. Now that I understand what the Bible teaches about death, I think of it as going to sleep in my heavenly Father's strong arms. That's a secure and peaceful thought for me.

5. Ted

When I have a fitful sleep, the night seems long and hard. But when I have a peaceful sleep, it seems no time has passed at all from when I fell asleep until I awoke the next morning. I think death and the resurrection will be much like that. One moment I will breathe out my last breath; the next moment of consciousness I will be awakened by Jesus with no sense of the passage of time.

ACTIVITY (1)

Write out your testimony with regard to the truth about death and beyond. To get you started answer the following questions:

1. How did you first hear about this truth?

2. What process did you go through in coming to accept it?

3. What does it mean to you today?

4. If you grew up in the church, how do you believe this truth has
helped you over the years?

_____

_____

_____

_____

_____

_____

_____

D. Contagious Adventist Skills

Starting Conversations

In starting conversations on the subject of death, it is very important
to be sensitive to emotional issues that may be involved. Unless
you are aware of how emotionally loaded this subject is for many
people, you could misunderstand and misinterpret their reaction
to something you say. Where possible, follow their lead—i.e., allow
them to bring the subject up in the first place. However, that may not
always happen. Following are some sample situations and examples
of possible conversation starters for this subject. Always be watchful
for evidences of their emotional reaction to what you are saying.

1. **To someone grieving over the loss of a loved one:**

   "I remember when my _____ died. It was really hard. Something the Bible says about death was a big help to me during that time, and still is."

2. **To someone who is NOT grieving over a recent loss:**

   "What do you think happens to someone when they die?" "What was it that led you to your understanding on that?" "Would you like to know what the Bible says about death?"

3. **To someone who may be recounting a spiritualism type movie they have seen:**

   "That stuff can be really scary. I am just so glad to know that the Bible teaches that the dead cannot come back to 'haunt' us. Isn't that reassuring?"

4. **If you know they are interested in psychics:**

   You could ask, "Do you think psychics can really communicate with the dead?" After they answer, you could say something like, "I've found some definitive comments on that subject in the Bible."

5. **When some highly noted person dies:**

   You might say, "Have you ever noticed that almost all funeral talks make some reference to the deceased being in heaven or in a better place now?" After they answer, you could say something like, "A lot of people would be surprised if they knew what the Bible actually taught about what happens when someone dies."

6. **After attending a funeral or just initiating a conversation about death and beyond:**

   "Many funeral sermons say that the dead person is in heaven now. If that is true, have you ever wondered why the Bible speaks about a resurrection that will take place at the end of the world? Why would God need to resurrect people who are already in heaven?"

E. Asking for a Decision

1. Guidelines for asking for decisions:

a. Use a series of questions to determine the level of decision a person is ready to make.

b. Always begin with general questions to determine their understanding of the subject and if they need further information. If more is needed, make arrangements to provide it before proceeding to the next level.

c. Proceed from one level of questions to another as long as you continue to get a positive response. When you do not get a positive response, you can say something like, "Thanks for sharing your thoughts on this. I'll keep you in my thoughts and prayers."

d. Based on their responses to the questions you have asked, prayerfully determine an appropriate "next step" for them. No matter how they answer the questions you ask, there is always some appropriate "next step."

e. After you ask a question, wait for an answer. Do not be afraid of silence. Silence creates a vacuum. If you do not break it the other person will. They will likely answer your question directly or indirectly.

f. It may be that the person does not have an answer at that time, but the very fact that they have heard the question is like a seed being planted. They will think about it. God will bring it to their mind at the appropriate times.

2. Progressive Levels of Questions:

After you have presented the Bible truth and your own testimony regarding the truth about death, the following list of progressively escalating questions will help you determine the level of decision a person is ready to make. When multiple options are provided, they will be indicated by numbers. (They are not progressive.) Pray that the Holy Spirit will guide you in determining the most appropriate option, which may be different than those suggested. And remember, regardless of what the immediate results appear to be, the Holy Spirit will always use such conversations to His advantage to reach hearts for eternity. Trust in God and He will ensure that your faithful efforts bear fruit.

	Question(s) for a Christian	Question(s) for a Non-Christian
Level 1: Understanding Grasp of the truth about death	1. "Does what I've shared about what happens when someone dies make sense to you?" 2. "Do you have any questions about how I understand what the Bible teaches about death?"	1. "Does what I've shared about what happens when someone dies make sense to you?" 2. "Do you understand why I believe this subject is so important?"
Level 2: Desire Sense of personal need for the benefit that the truth about death could add to their life	1. "Can you see how someone who clearly understands death as an unconscious sleep would be protected from the deception of the occult?" 2. "Isn't it consoling to know that our dead loved ones are sleeping peacefully in Jesus, unaware of all the evil, suffering, and trials that are happening on earth?"	1. "Can you see that the Bible teaching about death being an unconscious sleep means that the occult world and séances are not based on real communication with dead relatives, but is a rather great deception based on a real spiritual realm of evil that exists?" 2. "Can you see how consoling it is to know that our deceased loved ones don't have to watch all the suffering taking place in our world today?"

	Question(s) for a Christian	Question(s) for a Non-Christian
Level 3: Conviction How strongly they feel it is important to act on truth about death	"Can you see how important it is to believe that death is a sleep as the Bible teaches, so that we can help warn unsuspecting people about the dangers of attempting to communicate with the dead?"	"Don't you think it's important to know what will happen to us after we die, especially if there's a chance that there will be a resurrection from the dead, and that our eternal destiny would depend on how we relate to what the Bible says we must do in this life to gain eternal life as opposed to eternal death?"
Next Step Appropriate follow-up action they, or you, might take in support of their spiritual journey, based on your perception of their readiness to accept it	1. "Would you be interested in learning more about this subject? I have a great book I could lend you." (For example: *Living Lies About Death and the Hereafter* by Henry Feyerabend) 2. "Would you be interested in coming over to my house some evening for some refreshments and to watch a really good video that explains this further?" (For example: any video on death filmed during an evangelistic series)	1. "Would you be interested in learning more about this subject? I have a great book I could lend you." (For example: *Living Lies About Death and the Hereafter* by Henry Feyerabend) 2. "Would you be interested in coming over to my house some evening for some refreshments and to watch a really good video that explains this further?" (For example: any video on death filmed during an evangelistic series)

3. Decision Texts Related to the Truth About Death

a. "Then the serpent said to the woman, 'You will not surely die.'"
   Genesis 3:4

b. "Behold, all souls are Mine; the soul of the father as well
   as the soul of the son is Mine; the soul who sins shall die."
   Ezekiel 18:4 NKJV

c. "For in death there is no remembrance of You; in the grave
   who will give You thanks?" "The dead do not praise the LORD,
   nor any who go down into silence." Psalm 6:5; 115:17 NKJV

d. "Do not marvel at this, for the hour is coming in which all who
   are in the graves will hear his voice and come forth—those who
   have done good, to the resurrection of life, and those who have
   done evil, to the resurrection of condemnation."
   John 5:28–29 NKJV

   "He who has the Son has life; he who does not have the Son of
   God does not have life." 1 John 5:12

 VIDEO

E. HOMEWORK

1. **Read the preview for Session 6,** the biblical truth perfectly
   designed to satisfy the human hunger for hope.

2. Be alert to the openings that God will provide for you this week
   to share the good news about what happens when people die.
   Have the courage to open your mouth and share in a contagious
   way. Remember, when someone tells you that a dead person is in
   heaven, they are sharing their theology. Do not hesitate: Should
   not we who know the Lord declare what we believe?

PREVIEW FOR SESSION 6: THE SECOND COMING

"Prisoners of Hope"

The increasing secularization of western society arouses a deep hunger that longs to be satisfied—a hunger for hope.

That deep-seated hunger for hope may be the reason that *Left Behind*, the fictitious book series on how the world will end, stands as the best-selling book series of all time. People want assurance that there will be a happy ending. They are "prisoners of hope" (Zechariah 9:12).

The Bible describes people who are "without hope and without God in the world" (Ephesians 2:12). The clear message is, if you find God, you find hope. Those who seek God and have a relationship with God can be assured of a happy ending.

"The Blessed Hope"

The great hope God offers the world is the return of His Son Jesus. Paul aptly expressed the believer's greatest longing: "We wait for the blessed hope—the glorious appearing of our great God and Savior, Jesus Christ" (Titus 2:13).

On the eve of His passion, Jesus Himself promised: "In my Father's house are many rooms....I am going there to prepare a place for you. And if I go and prepare a place for you, I will come back and take you to be with me that you also may be where I am" (John 14:2–3).

The Second Coming of Jesus is one of the most referred to teachings in all of Scripture—over 1,500 places in the Bible, including one in every 25 verses in the New Testament. For every Old Testament prophecy of His first coming, there are eight prophecies of His Second Coming. His return is the great and grand climax toward which the entire Bible story moves. The Bible fittingly ends with the prayer, "Come, Lord Jesus" (Revelation 22:20).

Millions of believers through the millenniums of earth's history have been sustained through times of immense suffering by the assurance that in the end Jesus will return to make all things right and to take them to be with Him for eternity (2 Corinthians 4:16–18). It is the great light at the end of the tunnel.

The Nature of His Return

Jesus warned that imposters would impersonate His return "and will deceive many" (Matthew 24:4–5, 24). His warning makes the Bible's description of *how* He will return important to understand. Jesus' return will be:

- Highly visible and noisy, like lightning flashing from east to west. (Matthew 24:24–27)

- Powerful and glorious as He returns on the clouds of heaven. (Matthew 24:30)

- Universally witnessed and experienced. (Revelation 1:7)

- Joyous and triumphant as saved loved ones are resurrected and reunited. (1 Thessalonians 4:15–16)

Based on these texts, it is obvious that the Second Coming of Jesus will not be a quiet arrival or a secret departure of the saints.

Jesus Himself eagerly anticipates the day when He will return and take us to be with Him. Just as a bride and groom want their friends to be present at their wedding, and new parents want their friends to see their new baby, Jesus wants all heaven to be present when He returns to gather His trusting children to Him. "When the Son of Man comes in his glory and *all the angels with him...*" (Matthew 25:31). He can hardly wait!

The Time of His Return

Jesus' disciples asked Him the question every believer longs to have answered: How can we know when Your return is getting near? (Matthew 24:3). Jesus did not give an exact date for His return, but neither did He dodge the question of His coming. He gave signs by which we could know the time was near:

- Wars would increase. (Matthew 24:6–7)

- Famines would intensify. (Matthew 24:7)

- Pestilences (diseases) and earthquakes would increase. (Matthew 24:7)

- Lawlessness and lovelessness would increase. (Matthew 24:12)

- There would be great increases in knowledge and travel. (Daniel 12:4)

Anyone who watched CNN for 24 hours would see evidences for each of the signs Jesus gave us. And He said, "'when you see all these things, know that it is near—at the doors!'" (Matthew 24:33 NKJV)

Jesus has wanted His people to be ever expectant, as though He might return at any time soon, and thus to be always prepared. In the last book of the Bible, as kind of a grand finale, He is quoted three times saying: "'I am coming soon'" (Revelation 22:7, 12, 20). His point? "'Be on guard! Be alert! You do not know when that time will come'" (Mark 13:33).

How to Prepare

As exciting and wonderful as Jesus' return will be for those who are prepared for it, it will be equally though oppositely awful for those who are not. Those who have spurned God's efforts to woo them and draw them into a saving relationship with Him will cry in terror at His return, for they will realize what an incredible opportunity they have squandered (Matthew 16:26–27). And contrary to what some teach, we have only this life to get it right. There is no second chance. "Man is destined to die once, and after that to face judgment" (Hebrews 9:27).

Jesus said that if we put our trust in Him, repent of our sins, and submit to His Lordship and leadership in our lives, we will not perish (Luke 13:3, 5; John 3:16). He said, "'Watch and pray...that you may be able to stand before the Son of Man'" (Luke 21:36). To "watch" means to take God seriously. To "pray" means to ask Him to take control of your life and to glorify Himself through you on a daily basis.

Anyone who thus takes even the first step toward Jesus can rest in His incredible assurance: "'...whoever comes to me I will never drive away'" (John 6:37). They have found "the blessed hope!"

Session 6

The Second Coming: The Blessed Hope

In this session we will:

1. Study the sequence of events initiated by the Second Coming.

2. Answer questions about the rapture.

3. Outline and share your personal testimony related to the Second Coming.

4. Recognize and create Contagious Adventist Moments.

5. Learn how to ask for decisions related to the Second Coming.

A. Human Beings Hunger for Hope

1. What is life ultimately all about?

   a. When we get into the school we applied to, what then?

   b. When we get that degree we worked so hard for, what then?

   c. When we get that job we had our hearts set on, what then?

   d. When we marry the perfect person we dreamed of, what then?

   e. When we have our first child, what then?

   f. When we get our children educated and married off, what then?

   g. When we retire with the portfolio we spent 40 years building, what then?

   h. When we come to the end, as every one of us inevitably will, what then? (When we die, what then?)

2. As Christians we have hope:

   a. Hope of seeing _____ face to face and hearing Him say, "Welcome Home." (Revelation 21:3–4)

   b. Hope of being _____ with loved ones who sleep in Jesus. (1 Thessalonians 4:14–17)

   c. Hope for a _____ world as God originally planned where there will be no more war, violence, injustice, sickness, and death. (Isaiah 4:2; 11:6; Revelation 21:3–4)

   d. Hope for a glorious future that has no _____. (2 Corinthians 4:16–18)

B. Sequence of Events Initiated by the Second Coming:

1. All the inhabitants of the world will see and hear Jesus coming back in the clouds of heaven, glorified as King of kings and Lord of lords, and all the holy angels with Him. (Matthew 25:31; Revelation 1:7; 19:16)

2. The righteous who have died will be resurrected from their graves and taken to Heaven. They will be resurrected in the strength and beauty of their youth, never to grow old and die again. (1 Corinthians 15:51–54; 1 Thessalonians 4:16)

3. The unrighteous who have died will remain dead until the 1,000 years are ended. (Revelation 20:5)

4. The righteous who are living will be joined in joyful reunion with those who have been resurrected, and together they will experience the thrill of ascending from this earth to meet Jesus in the air. (1 Thessalonians 4:17)

5. The unrighteous that are living will perish. The earth will be desolate and devoid of all human life, violence, and suffering. (There is no seven-year grace period for the unrighteous.) (Revelation 19:11–21)

6. Jesus will take His believing children to be with Him in the heavenly Jerusalem for 1,000 years. (The millennium will take place in heaven, not on the earth.) (1 Thessalonians 4:17; Revelation 20:6)

   During this thousand-year period in heaven, "the saints will judge the world"—examine the judgment records and have the awesome privilege of having all their questions answered by God Himself. They will come to understand the wisdom and compassion of God's judgment and they will be at peace with all of God's decisions and actions. (1 Corinthians 6:2–3; Revelation 20:4)

7. Satan and his angels will be confined to "the Abyss" or "bottomless pit"—the earth in its desolate, uninhabited condition—for 1,000 years, unable to tempt or inflict pain and suffering on anyone during that time. (The term "millennium" does not occur in the Bible, but is the Latin term that refers to the thousand-year period mentioned specifically only in Revelation 20.) (Jeremiah 4:23; Revelation 20:1–2)

8. After the 1,000 years Jesus will bring His believing children and the heavenly Jerusalem down to this earth. (Revelation 21:2)

9. God will resurrect the unrighteous dead. By this act God will release Satan from his thousand-year confinement, freeing him to tempt and lead those who followed him during their lives on earth. Satan, his angels, and all the unrighteous will see the glory of God, understand the depth of their sin/rebellion, confess that Jesus Christ is indeed Lord of all, yet remain unrepentant. They will attempt to storm the city of God and will be defeated and cast into the lake of fire to be annihilated forever. This is the second death—the eternal death from which there is no resurrection. Sin and sinners will be no more. (Psalm 37:10; Isaiah 45:23; Ezekiel 28:13–15,18–19; Obadiah 16; Philippians 2:10; Revelation 20:3, 5, 7–10; 21:8)

10. The earth will be recreated as more beautiful than it had been in the Garden of Eden, and God's believing, faithful children will dwell in Paradise Restored with their Redeemer for all eternity. (Isaiah 11:6–9; 35:1–10; Matthew 5:5; 2 Peter 3:10–13; Revelation 21:3–7)

Sequence of events initiated by the Second Coming

	Dead	Those who are alive	During the 1,000 years	End of the 1,000 years
Righteous	• Raised Rev. 20:6 1 Thess. 4:15–16 • Taken to heaven	• Taken to heaven 1 Thess. 4:17 Rev. 20:4	• Will judge the world Rev. 20:4	• Return to earth with heavenly Jerusalem Rev. 21:1-2 • Will live forever 1 Thess. 4:15–17 Rev. 21:3–4; 22:5 • Paradise will be restored Rev. 21:1-4; 22:1-5
Unrighteous	• Remain dead until the 1,000 years are ended Rev. 20:5	• Slain at the brightness of Jesus' coming 2 Thess. 1:5–10; 2:8	• Satan and the unrighteous dead are confined to this earth Rev. 20:1-3, 7 Gen. 1:1-2 Jer. 4:23-27	• Resurrected Rev. 20:5, 7–8 • Confess that Jesus is Lord yet remain unrepentant Phil. 2:9–11, Rev. 20:7-9 • Destroyed in the lake of fire Rev. 20:9–10, 14 • Sin and sinners will be no more Rev. 21:4, 8 Nahum 1:9

The biblical scenario we have just looked at is greatly different from the "rapture" teaching that became popular in the *Left Behind* book series.

Let us look at some of the Contagious Adventist Moments that may arise because of the secret rapture ideas.

C. Questions About the Rapture

1. Question: I've been reading one of the *Left Behind* books. It sounds spooky to me that planes will be left without pilots flying them and things like that. How fair is that to the passengers?

Possible Answers:

a. That teaching is called the "rapture." It was not taught in Christianity until the 19th century when John Nelson Darby, an Anglican preacher, developed the idea. Darby taught that Jesus would return secretly to rapture His true followers, leaving the rest to be ruled by an evil antichrist for seven years. The teaching states that during that time there would be great persecution and many Jews, and others who had not taken God seriously before the rapture, would become believers and be saved. Then Jesus would return again to take them to heaven and assign all remaining unbelievers to hell.

Cyrus Scofield later published a Bible that promoted Darby's views on the rapture in its explanatory notes. The Scofield Bible is still very popular today.

The *Left Behind* book series has popularized the rapture theory. But that theory is not taught in the Bible.

b. The Bible describes the Second Coming of Jesus as the most dramatic, electrifying, wonderful (if you're prepared), and terrifying (if you're not) event in our planet's history. In fact it says clearly that every person alive on earth will see Him coming (Revelation 1:7). And the graves of believers who have ever lived throughout history will be opened and all those resurrected will ascend into the sky to meet Jesus

(1 Thessalonians 4:16–17). There's no hint in the Bible that Jesus' coming will be in secret or stealth! So no one has to worry about whether the plane they are flying will suddenly be without a pilot. A much bigger concern is whether they are ready to meet Jesus when He does come.

2. **Question:** The Bible says somewhere that when Jesus comes two men will be working in the field and one will be taken and the other left. Doesn't that mean that one will be taken to be with God and the other one left here on earth just like the rapture theory teaches?

Possible Answer:

People who refer to Matthew 24:40–41 and Luke 17:34–37 to support the rapture theory teach that some will be "taken" to heaven, and others will be "left behind" to continue living on this earth for a period of time (up to seven years) before Jesus' Second Coming. But the Bible presents a different picture.

The verses in question simply say that when Jesus comes, two will be working side by side, or will be lying in bed side by side, and that one of them will be ready to meet Jesus and will go to heaven with Him, and the other will not be, but will be destroyed.

Different Bible interpreters have argued whether those Jesus said would be "taken" would be taken to heaven or taken to be destroyed. Even the disciples asked the question, "Where Lord?" In other words, Where will those you take be taken to? Jesus "replied, 'Where there is a dead body, the vultures will gather'" (Luke 17:34–37). Instead of answering the disciples' question directly, His cryptic answer assured them that the final judgment will be certain and universal. When and where it happens, it will be as obvious as the sight of birds of prey circling in the sky indicating that some animal is dying and about to be devoured. In fact, the book of Revelation actually says that those who are not ready for Jesus to come will die and be devoured by birds of prey (Revelation 19:17–18, 21). It is a very sobering picture.

When Jesus taught that at His Second Coming one would be taken and the other left, He was warning everyone that on the final Day of Judgment two people who may be very close as friends or family will be separated forever if one of them has a relationship with Him and the other does not. One will be received by Jesus to live with Him forever, while the other will be eternally lost. That is another reason why it is important for us to be Contagious Adventists and to share Jesus' love with everyone we know and love, so that such a separation might never occur between us.

Not only does the Bible not teach that some will be taken to heaven before others, it actually disputes it. First Thessalonians 4:16–17 says that those who are alive when Jesus comes will not go to be with Jesus ahead of those who died believing in Jesus. It says *they will "be caught up together"* to meet Jesus and to be with Him forever.

And when this happens there will certainly not be anything secret about it, like half the world would wake up some morning and find out Jesus came quietly in the night and took the other half of the world to heaven. In those same chapters where Jesus said one would be taken and the other left, Jesus said His coming "will be like the lightning, which flashes and lights up the sky from one end to the other" (Matthew 24:27; Luke 17:24). And Revelation 1:7 says "every eye will see him."

3. **Question:** What difference does it make if someone believes in the rapture theory of Jesus' return?

Possible Answer:

The rapture theory teaches that when Jesus comes the second time, the righteous will be "taken" to heaven and the unrighteous will be "left behind" on the earth for another seven years until Jesus comes the third time for the final judgment. In other words, if you are not ready for Jesus' Second Coming, you will still have time to get ready for His third coming seven years later.

This is a very dangerous teaching. It implies that someone could put off making a decision to follow God today, and if they are not ready for the "rapture," they will still have a second chance to get it right. This is a dangerous teaching and could be fatal to one's chances for eternal life. Millions of people who rely on the rapture theory may be counting on a second chance to turn to God, a second chance that does not exist! The Bible says, "Be reconciled to God... now is the day of salvation" (2 Corinthians 5:20; 6:2). "Today, if you hear his voice, do not harden your hearts..." (Hebrews 3:15). Delay is never advocated, and procrastination is portrayed as dangerous and tantamount to disaster. By the time a person dies, their decision will have been irrevocably made for or against God—there is no second chance after death. "... man is destined to die once, and after that to face judgment..." (Hebrews 9:12). Similarly, before Jesus returns at His Second Coming every person still living will have made their decision irrevocably for or against God—there will be no second chance after Jesus returns (Revelation 22:11–12). About that the Bible is unmistakably clear.

 VIDEO

D. Personal Testimonies

1. Rich

I grew up in a church that believed the doctrine of Jesus' Second Coming but didn't talk much about it. Sunday sermons usually focused on living honorably, with appeals to believe in Jesus. A Seventh-day Adventist friend and I often discussed world events and trials in our own lives. He talked a lot about the Second Coming of Jesus and seemed so hopeful. At first his attitude seemed unreal to me but as he showed me Bible texts about the Second Coming it brought a ray of hope to my own life. I began to realize that my trials are only temporary. A better day is ahead— Jesus is coming again!

2. Reggie

Life just couldn't get any better. I was in a thriving law practice. I'd been married for less than a year and was still in the honeymoon stage. Yet I often wondered why I was so favored and others weren't. I realized my life didn't have an ultimate purpose. Then I read a book on the end of the world and it got me thinking. I had grown up without religion and had done quite well. But it did make sense that there would be some kind of accounting at the end of life. I bought a Bible and read it for the first time in my life. It confirmed what I had been feeling—there will be a final reckoning at the end of the world. After months of discussion and Bible lessons with an Adventist colleague, I was baptized into the Adventist church. The Bible teaching of the Second Coming has given real purpose to my life. No matter how favored I am here, I know I'm only passing through on the way to my true home. Now as a lawyer my job is not only to help people get a fair hearing in court, but to use my influence and favored status to help others set their hopes on the better world to come.

3. Lisa

I grew up in a Christian home. But when I went away to college, my life turned in another direction. I'm ashamed of all the places that lifestyle took me. For a long time I enjoyed my new life and was grateful to be liberated from my sheltered upbringing. But every once in a while, out of nowhere, something would remind me that Jesus was going to come back. I tried to get that thought out of my mind but eventually it overwhelmed me. I don't think I would be a Christian today if it weren't for the teaching I had as a child that Jesus is coming back. That truth brought me back to God. I will be forever grateful for the power of this Bible teaching.

4. Enoch

The belief that Jesus will come again influences every day of my life. It wasn't always that way, but since I asked Jesus to be the Lord of my life, hardly a day passes that I don't think about actually seeing Him face to face someday. It's a joy I try to share with everyone I can. I can hardly wait. I can't imagine any relative or friend of mine missing out on that experience.

5. Doug

I grew up in a conservative evangelical church and got "saved" when I was ten. I didn't always live a very good life, but I didn't worry about it because I believed that since I had been saved it would all turn out okay in the end. I believed that if the rapture occurred in my lifetime, I'd be among those taken up. I became friends with a Seventh-day Adventist who talked a lot about the Second Coming of Jesus. Eventually I realized that some of the ideas I had about Jesus' Second Coming weren't what the Bible teaches. But the thing that got to me most was when my friend showed me something Jesus said in the Sermon on the Mount. Jesus said that many people who think they're ready to meet Him when He returns will be sadly surprised to find out that they aren't. My friend told me that he prays for Jesus to protect him from being deceived like that. Then he asked me if I ever had doubts about whether I would be ready to meet Jesus when He comes. Actually, I hadn't really thought about it since I believed I had been saved. But I couldn't get that Bible verse and question out of my mind. Eventually God used that conversation to help me realize that I needed to depend more on Him every day than on some experience I thought I had when I was ten. It helped me come into a much closer relationship with God. Now I can honestly say that I do look forward to Jesus' Second Coming more than ever before. And I've learned that as I depend on Him and trust Him daily, He will keep me safe until that day.

E. Contagious Adventist Skills

1. Sharing your testimony

ACTIVITY (1) (2)

Outline your testimony regarding the Second Coming.

Think of ways the truth about the Second Coming of Jesus has impacted your life:

a. It may be a general, overall impact.

b. You may remember a particular time, such as at a death, when that truth gave you great hope.

c. It may be some wonderful experience you had that made you think of the never-ending joys of heaven and the new earth.

d. It may be the expectation of meeting Jesus face to face, etc.

_____

_____

_____

_____

_____

_____

2. Recognizing and Creating Contagious Adventist Moments

a. Any experience related to hardship in someone's life.

For example:

1) If the person you are talking with has experienced a loss:

"I feel bad that you hurt so deeply right now. It makes me look forward to the Second Coming of Jesus even more."

Then watch to see if they give indication that they would like your conversation to continue in that direction.

2) If the person you are talking with is severely ill or handicapped:

"Don't you look forward to the day when there will be no more sickness or suffering?" "Don't you look forward to the day when our bodies will be restored to their perfect state?"

Pray that their response will let you know clearly whether they are ready to talk about that day more.

3) If you hear people talking about AIDS, SARS, etc.:

"I'm so glad that diseases like that will someday be a thing of the past. Did you know that the Bible actually promises that?"

b. **When you're having a great time with someone:**

"You know, we think this is good...! But there's a day coming that will be a thousand times better!"

c. **At a school or family reunion:**

"Think of the incredible reunion we will have when Jesus returns—no more aging, hair loss, weight gain, or hard and long separations from family and friends."

d. **If you are talking with someone reading a book in the *Left Behind* series:**

"Are you a student of the Bible yourself, or is your understanding of the Second Coming of Jesus based primarily on that book?" "Have you ever read what the Bible says about Jesus' return? There are some amazing differences between what the Bible teaches and the *Left Behind* series."

e. **Articles in *Newsweek*, *Time*, etc.** frequently use the term **"Armageddon"** when referring to a looming conflict in the Middle East. Use an article or newspaper reference as a starter: "Did you notice that article in...talking about Armageddon? A lot of people talk about Armageddon, but not many know what the Bible says about it. Have you ever read about Armageddon in the Bible?" While this is not the easiest subject to discuss, you do not need to have all the answers. Simply note that the Bible associates Armageddon with the end of the world and the Second Coming of Jesus (Revelation 16:16–21 is the only direct reference to Armageddon in the Bible). This opens the door to share the hope offered in the Second Coming of Jesus for all who trust in Him and are seeking to obey Him.

f. **If someone you are close to escaped death from a serious illness or accident:**

"I'm so thankful that God spared your life and has given you more time. Have you considered whether you would have been ready to meet Him if your life had been taken?" If you have had a near brush with death, share how that was a wake-up call for you to realize the importance of being ready to meet God at any time.

F. Asking for a Decision

1. Guidelines for Asking for Decisions:

a. Use a series of questions to determine the level of decision a person is ready to make.

b. Always begin with general questions to determine their understanding of the subject and if they need further information. If more is needed, make arrangements to provide it before proceeding to the next level.

c. Proceed from one level of questions to another as long as you continue to get a positive response. When you do not get a positive response, you can say something like, "Thanks for sharing your thoughts on this. I'll keep you in my thoughts and prayers."

d. Based on their responses to the questions you have asked, prayerfully determine an appropriate "next step" for them. No matter how they answer the questions you ask, there is always some appropriate "next step."

e. After you ask a question, wait for an answer. Do not be afraid of silence. Silence creates a vacuum. If you do not break it the other person will. They will likely answer your question directly or indirectly.

f. It may be that the person does not have an answer at that time, but the very fact that they have heard the question is like a seed being planted. They will think about it. God will bring it to their mind at the appropriate times.

2. Progressive Levels of Questions:

After you have presented the Bible truth and your own testimony regarding the Second Coming of Jesus, the following list of progressively escalating questions will help you determine the level of decision a person is ready to make. When multiple options are provided, they will be indicated by numbers. (These are not progressive.) Pray that the Holy Spirit will guide you in determining the most appropriate option, which may be different than those suggested. And remember, regardless of what the immediate results appear to be, the Holy Spirit will always use such conversations to His advantage to reach hearts for eternity. Trust in God and He will ensure that your faithful efforts bear fruit.

	Question(s) for a Christian	Question(s) for a Non-Christian
Level 1: Understanding Grasp of the truth about Jesus' Second Coming (includes the biblical truth and your personal testimony related to it)	1. "Does what I've shared about the Second Coming of Jesus match what you understand the Scriptures teach regarding it?" 2. "Do you have any questions about my understanding of what the Bible teaches about Jesus' Second Coming?"	1. "Does what I've shared about the Second Coming of Jesus make sense to you?" 2. "Can you see why my understanding of the Second Coming of Jesus gives me such hope?" 3. "Do you have any questions about the Second Coming of Jesus?"
Level 2: Desire Sense of personal need for the benefit that Jesus' Second Coming could add to their life	1. "When you think about the Second Coming of Jesus, what is it that you look forward to the most?" Possible follow-up response and question: "That's interesting. Why do you look forward to that the most?" 2. "Isn't it reassuring to know that Jesus told us in advance how He would return so that we wouldn't be deceived by some impersonation attempt by the evil one?"	1. "Does what I've shared about the Second Coming of Jesus appeal to you?" 2. "Does what I've shared about the Second Coming of Jesus make you want to be ready to meet Him when He returns?" 3. "Do you ever long to experience the biblical description of the new world Jesus is preparing for us?" (e.g., universal peace, no suffering, authentic and loving relationships that do not go sour, meeting God face to face)

	Question(s) for a Christian	Question(s) for a Non-Christian
Level 3: Conviction How strongly they feel it is important to act on the issues related to Jesus' Second Coming	"Can you see how someone who clearly understands what the Bible teaches about Jesus' Second Coming would be protected from many potential deceptions regarding it?" (that some people will have a second chance to get it right after Jesus returns, that Jesus would show up somewhere in secret or on television rather than in the clouds for all to see, etc.)	1. "Do you have a desire to be ready to meet Jesus when He returns to take His followers to be with Him for eternity?" 2. "Is there anything in your life right now that you are aware of that might prevent you from being ready to meet Jesus when He comes?"
Next Step Appropriate follow-up action they, or you, might take in support of their spiritual journey, based on your perception of their readiness to accept it	1. "Would you be interested in studying more about Jesus' Second Coming? I have a great book I could lend you." (Check your local ABC for a recent book on Jesus' Second Coming.) 2. "Would you be interested in studying more about this subject together? I have a great Bible study on this subject that we could go through together." 3. "Would you be interested in coming over to my house some evening for some refreshments and to watch a really good video that explains this further?" (For example: any evangelistic series video on the Second Coming or signs of Jesus' return)	1. "Would you be interested in learning more about Jesus' Second Coming and how to be ready for it? I have a great book I could lend you." (Check your local ABC.) 2. "Would you be interested in studying together more of what the Bible teaches about Jesus' Second Coming and how we can prepare for it?" 3. "Would you be interested in coming over to my house some evening for some refreshments and to watch a really good video that explains this further?" (For example: any evangelistic series video on the Second Coming or signs of Jesus' return)

3. Decision Texts Related to Jesus' Second Coming

a. "For God so loved the world that He gave His only begotten Son, that whoever believes in Him should not perish but have everlasting life. For God did not send His Son into the world to condemn the world, but that the world through Him might be saved. He who believes in Him is not condemned; but he who does not believe is condemned already, because he has not believed in the name of the only begotten Son of God." John 3:16–18 NKJV

b. "For it is by grace you have been saved, through faith—and this not from yourselves, it is the gift of God—not by works, so that no one can boast." Ephesians 2:9–10

c. "The grace of God that brings salvation has appeared to all men. It teaches us to say 'No' to ungodliness and worldly passions, and to live self-controlled, upright and godly lives in this present age, while we wait for the blessed hope—the glorious appearing of our great God and Savior, Jesus Christ, who gave himself for us to redeem us from all wickedness and to purify for himself a people that are his very own, eager to do what is good." Titus 2:11–14

ACTIVITY (3)

Think of the people on your impact list. From the list of conversation starters and questions, pick a question or scenario that you think you might engage in with someone on your impact list. Discuss your approach with a partner.

G. Homework

1. **Read preview for Session 7,** the truth designed to give us abundant life here and now.

2. This week, share your contagious Adventist testimony about the Second Coming with someone and report to the group next week.

PREVIEW FOR SESSION 7: HEALTH

A Generation Obsessed With Health

We live in a generation obsessed with health. Millions of people pursue one fad diet regimen after another and engage in one exercise routine after another in a desperate attempt to lose weight or achieve a healthy heart. Some do so with a genuine interest in health, while others do so just to appear more attractive and are even willing to jeopardize their health in hopes of looking more attractive or of performing better (as is the case with much cosmetic plastic surgery, breast implants, tanning salons, steroids, etc.). On the other hand, many people are willing to ignore the laws of health, excusing themselves with the belief that modern medicine can fix anything. But everyone wants good health and a long, happy life. In short, they want to really live!

Set Free to Really Live

Jesus once met a crippled woman whom He described as "a daughter of Abraham, whom Satan has kept bound for eighteen long years" (Luke 13:16). Characteristically, He set her free from her bondage. He loved to heal people and set them free to really live.

Satan's hatred for God manifests itself in attacks on His children (Job 1–2; Revelation 12:17). He afflicts them not only through sufferings imposed from without on the innocent, but also through choices people voluntarily make that enslave them to various addictions and unhealthy lifestyles that result in dire consequences of ill health, physically and spiritually. But Jesus still loves to heal people and set them free to really live (John 10:10).

Christian Stewardship

The Apostle John's prayer for his fellow believers was "that you may enjoy good health and that all may go well with you" (3 John 2). That is God's desire for His children. But not all Christians have good health. Sometimes God allows circumstances that prevent good health, as when babies are born with rare forms of cancer and live a few years at best. Such scenarios are practically endless. Even when Jesus was here He did not heal all the unhealthy people in the world. Some of these things will remain mysteries until He explains them in the new earth.

You have heard the adages: "If you have your health, you have just about everything," and "The goal of life is to die young, as late in life as possible." Well, they are only partially true. Many godly martyrs chose to die young rather than to deny their faith. According to the Bible, the goal of life is not good health and long life at all costs, but rather faithfulness to God even if it should lead to a shorter life (Matthew 5:11–12; 1 Corinthians 4:2).

But much ill health and premature death results from self-inflicted causes and can be prevented. Where this is the case, health becomes a spiritual issue. It is a matter of Christian stewardship.

"Do you not know that your body is a temple of the Holy Spirit, who is in you, whom you have received from God? You are not your own; you were bought at a price. Therefore honor God with your body." (1 Corinthians 6:19–20)

"So whether you eat or drink or whatever you do, do it all for the glory of God." (1 Corinthians 10:31)

Those who have chosen to follow Jesus as the Lord of their lives will try to live as healthy as they can. Obeying God's laws of health as revealed in the Bible and through nature protects us from some unnecessary and preventable illness, aids recovery from sickness when it does occur, and opens the way for deeper communion with God through the Holy Spirit (Exodus 15:26; 23:25; 1 Corinthians 6:19). If you have ever tried to spend meaningful time with God in study and prayer when you had a fever of 101 degrees or were severely fatigued, you know that good health and a keen mind are aids to communion with God.

Ultimate Issues in Healthy Living

According to the Bible, the ultimate issues in healthy living are not physical, but relational and spiritual—loving service to others and trusting in God. It affirms that in God's eyes, and thus in the eyes of His children, people are more important than food (Matthew 11:19; 1 Corinthians 10:27). In fact, loving service to people in need is an important component of the Bible's prescription for healing (Isaiah 58:6–9).

The National Institute of Healthcare Research has reviewed over 300 research studies on the influence of religion and spirituality on physical health. Psychologists Kevin S. Seybold and Peter C. Hill compiled the results in a chart showing the "Salutary effects of religion and spirituality" on fifteen standard health indicators including blood pressure, heart disease, cholesterol levels, stroke, longevity, etc. On the whole, in every single category, those who practiced an active spiritual faith were healthier and lived longer ("The Role of Religion and Spirituality in Mental and Physical Health," *Current Directions in Psychological Science*, Vol. 10, No. 1, February 2001, 21–24). No drug or medical procedure known to humanity, no healthy habit, can produce such results.

The ultimate goal of life is not physical health for the purpose of living a few more years on this earth. "For the kingdom of God is not a matter of eating and drinking, but of righteousness, peace and joy in the Holy Spirit..." (Romans 14:17).

Many people are investing enormous amounts of time and money to improve their physical health simply to feel a little better and live a few years longer on this earth, while ignoring the spiritual message of the Bible which offers an infinitely greater hope. "For physical training is of some value, but godliness has value for all things, holding promise for both this present life and the life to come" (1 Timothy 4:8).

Session 7

Health: God's Prescription

In this session we will:

1. Explore the biblical truth that can provide us with the most abundant life here and now through the practice of the Bible's health message.

2. Learn the **NEWSTART** ® acronym in order to share health principles.

3. Outline and share your testimony related to health.

4. Learn the skills needed to use this subject as a Contagious Adventist.

5. Practice Contagious Adventist skills with a partner.

6. Learn how to ask for a decision related to health.

A. Adventism's Timely/Timeless Health Message

1. What evidences do you see that our nation/our generation is obsessed with health?

_____

_____

_____

2. Why have a "health message"?

Through the health message God aimed to remove barriers to His communication to us, "for it is impossible for men and women, with all their sinful, health-destroying, brain-enervating habits, to discern sacred truth, through which they are to be sanctified, refined, elevated, and made fit for the society of heavenly angels in the kingdom of God" (*Counsels on Diet and Foods*, p. 70).

B. God's Prescription for Optimum Health—the Adventist Health Message

"What" is the Adventist Health Message?

1. What it is **NOT**:

a. It is not "the _____."

Romans 14:17
1 Timothy 4:8

b. It is not a guarantee of _____.

c. It does not assign _____ a higher value than

_____.

2. The Adventist health message is derived from God's prescription for optimum health given in Eden.

   "Pure air, sunlight, abstemiousness, rest, exercise, proper diet, the use of water, trust in divine power—these are the true remedies." *Ministry of Healing*, p. 127

3. This divine prescription for optimum health has been formulated into the Adventist health message under the acronym **NEWSTART ®** This term was coined and trademarked by Weimar College. Note this comment from their 2011 website:

   "Health Education
   Our bodies are the temple of God. Practicing the principles of good health ourselves helps us learn and think clearly, and enables us to communicate with God. We also seek to impart our knowledge of health to others. We firmly believe that health is the entering wedge of the gospel and so we have made health evangelism a major component of our program."

Here is the meaning of **NEWSTART ®**

		Divine Principles	Your Car
	N		
	E		
	W		
	S		
	T		
	A		
	R		
	T		

4. The **NEWSTART ®** formula for optimum health:

N _____

E _____

_____ to _____ minutes a day.

W _____

Your weight _____ lbs. divided by 2 = _____oz.

Divide by 8 to learn how many 8 oz. glasses to drink each day.

S _____

T _____

_____ from harmful things.

_____ in the use of healthy things.

A _____

R _____

_____ to _____ hours of sleep.

The _____, God's ordained weekly gift.

T _____

5. Some foods (e.g., pork) are forbidden by God for human consumption (Leviticus 11:1–19).

   a. The Bible establishes the principle of avoiding all harmful substances as part of our Christian stewardship and preparation for maximum communion with God (Proverbs 23:29–35).

   b. Daniel, a model for God's people living in the last days, "resolved not to defile himself with the royal food and wine" from the Babylonian king's table, but requested, "Give us nothing but vegetables to eat and water to drink" (Daniel 1:8, 12).

6. Modern scientific research has corroborated the value of the Bible's prescription for optimum health.

A major epidemiological study funded by the American Cancer Society and National Institute of Health, compared 35,000 Seventh-day Adventists living in California with the general population of that state.

On average,

SDA men lived_____ years longer, and

SDA women lived _____ years longer.

7. But again, the Adventist message is not simply about physical health, but about spiritual health/the gospel—Jesus is Lord, and He's coming back!

C. Contagious Adventist Skills

1. Testimonies

a. **Allen**

My first exposure to Seventh-day Adventists was their hospital in my hometown. I would drive by it every day on my way to work. One Saturday I was driving by an Adventist church and noticed cars in their parking lot. I slipped in for just a few minutes to see how they worshipped. I signed their guest book, and later that week I was visited by one of their elders. I asked if they practiced prayer for the sick, for my son was a cripple and had been told by medical authorities we had consulted that there was no hope he would ever walk. The elder said they did offer such prayer, and later brought me a little book by Ellen G. White entitled, Prayer for the Sick. *I later found that it was a chapter by that same name from another book she wrote entitled,* The Ministry of Healing. *I was impressed with that little book and wanted to know more about Ellen White. Three elders from their church came and prayed for my son and anointed him with oil. They began Bible studies with my family. I was the first one baptized. Later my family followed. Eight people in all have been baptized so far now among my family and friends. And thanks to medical treatment God opened up for us through which He provided His own healing grace, my son is walking today for the first time in his life. We have been abundantly blessed in every way.*

b. **Rachel**

Being raised as a Seventh-day Adventist, I've always had an interest in my health and have tried to live in a way that will give me the best chances for good health and a long and productive life. I can't say it's easy. I've struggled with weight issues for as long as I can remember, and probably will until the Lord comes. I've even tried a few of the faddish, quick-weight-loss programs which ended up being disillusioning and ineffective for me in the long run. There are so many conflicting claims these days as to what's the healthiest lifestyle. It can be so confusing. But over the years I've learned that the Bible's plan for my health can't be improved upon. I've learned to appreciate the simple plan God gave us that doesn't change with time and that seems to be confirmed with the latest scientific studies.

c. **Terry**

I used to smoke two and a half packs of cigarettes a day. I denied my addiction for a long time, believing I could quit whenever I wanted, and that smoking wasn't as harmful as people claimed. But I had a mild heart attack when I was in my early 40's and I took that as a wake-up call. Then I discovered the powerful hold cigarettes had on me. I tried for several years to quit, but with only minor success. I was still smoking over two packs a day when I heard about the Seventh-day Adventists' program on smoking. The teacher of our class invited people who needed extra help to stay by after class for prayer. I was desperate and stayed for prayer. I'm convinced that prayer is what gave me the victory. But then I got addicted to junk food as kind of a substitute. Again I prayed and asked some friends to pray for me also. And God is helping me with that. I still don't eat a perfect diet every day of my life; it's an ongoing challenge. But my life is so vastly improved from what it used to be. For me, the great value of the Adventist message wasn't just informing me of a healthy way to live. I already knew that I wasn't living in a way that was good for me. It was the emphasis on trust in God that gave me a new life. Even though I'm older now than I've ever been, I feel better than I've ever felt. I pray every day that God will protect me from ever falling back into the way that I used to live.

d. **Melissa**

I grew up in a Christian home, but I never really considered the things I ate or whether or not I exercised to be a spiritual issue. There was a work associate whom I admired for her cheerful attitude and positive outlook on life. I asked her how she got to be like that, and she told me that it was part of a health plan in the Bible. I had never heard of such a thing. As we talked further I found out that the Bible has a lot more to say about health than I ever imagined. The Adventist health message has been a blessing to me in so many ways. I enjoy my work more. And although I don't understand exactly how it works, I feel like I have better communication with God since I've been trying to live more healthfully.

ACTIVITY (1): Share your testimony of how one of these health principles has blessed your life.

2. Starting Conversations

a. Conversation starters occur naturally **when someone observes some element of your lifestyle.** For example, someone may say to you, "I notice that you don't order meat when we go out to eat." Or perhaps at a Rotary Club type meeting or on a plane: "How did you get that fruit plate? Did you call ahead and order it? Maybe I'll do that myself next time."

You could then explain that you do that for health purposes, but there is more than merely physical health involved. You believe that we will be better able to discern God's guidance in our lives if we have optimum health, and God's prescription for optimum health was established by God Himself in Eden—natural foods in their natural state. In Eden, before sin came, even the animals did not eat each other (Genesis 1:30). Then also explain the **NEWSTART ®** formula.

It is also important, however, to point out that someone does not have to be a vegetarian to accept Jesus or to become a Seventh-day Adventist. We must be very careful that we do not erect vegetarianism, or any component of the Adventist health message, as a barrier someone would have to cross before they felt they could accept Jesus and become His disciple.

b. Conversation starters can also occur **when someone makes a comment about some health issue in their own lifestyle.** For example, someone might remark about how tired they are all the time even though the doctor was not able to identify anything wrong. You might create a Contagious Adventist Moment by saying something like this: "Did you know that the Bible describes the original prescription for optimal health that God gave when He created human beings? Since God made us, His prescription for our health and happiness is like an owner's manual that describes how we can keep our bodies in the best running order." If they show an interest, you could review "God's Prescription for Optimum Health" as described in this session.

If they tell you, "I need to start exercising," you could invite them to walk with you.

c. You could **invite someone** to a Lifestyle Matters Seminar (produced by the Michigan Conference), a Breathe-Free stop smoking program, a nutrition and cooking class, a stress seminar, etc., sponsored by your church. Before you make the invitation, pray that your invitation will be received as a support to them, not as a criticism. The difference could make or break a relationship. You could say something like: "I'm going to a nutrition class. It would be more fun if you would go with me; we could do it together" or, "My friend, Jerry, went to this stop smoking program and quit. You've mentioned several times that you'd like to quit. You might find this program helpful." Even if they do not accept your invitation, perhaps because they are not ready to make the change yet, the manner in which the invitation is given could help them realize that you are a supportive friend, and bond your relationship closer than before.

d. Celebrity **connections.** Pay attention to reports of well-known people who have adopted some element of the Adventist health message. *Listen Magazine*, available from Adventist Book Centers, publishes just such stories about popular celebrities. Then when you are with someone whom you know admires that person, you could mention that you understand they have adopted that particular lifestyle element which is one advocated by God's original prescription for optimum health. If they express an interest in knowing more about it, you could describe the prescription as outlined in this session.

e. At **non-church potlucks** and other such **eating events** where people contribute food, bring a delicious and noticeable meatless dish and be prepared to explain why you brought a meatless dish if someone asks you.

f. Share **your own testimony** of how adopting God's original plan for optimum health has blessed you.

g. You could **offer to pray** for a friend or work colleague who has become sick.

h. If someone close to you is fighting a serious, perhaps life-threatening, disease, you could ask if they have heard about **the Bible's prayer for healing** that involves being anointed with oil. If they have, you could ask if their church (if they belong to one) has done this for them. If not, you might tell them about, or read to them, God's invitation to this prayer for healing in James 5:13–16. You could then offer to have one of the elders of your church come with you to talk to them about it. If they express an interest in knowing more, then call your pastor and see if s/he could go with you to talk to them about

it. This "Contagious Adventist Moment" should be reserved
for those you know quite well and who are suffering from a
serious illness. If they say they are not interested, nothing has
been lost on your part. But should they express an interest, it
could open the way for more discussions about spiritual issues,
as it did with Allen in our Testimonies section. And either
way, we have offered them an opportunity to take advantage
of a wonderful invitation God has extended for us to avail
ourselves of His special healing intervention—spiritually and/
or physically. While there is not always an immediate physical
healing, God promises His healing intervention at some level,
especially the spiritual ("If he has sinned, he will be forgiven";
James 5:15).

 VIDEO

ACTIVITY (2): Practice NEWSTART ®

D. Asking for a Decision

1. Guidelines for Asking for Decisions:

a. Use a series of questions to determine the level of decision a person is ready to make.

b. Always begin with general questions to determine their understanding of the subject and if they need further information. If more is needed, make arrangements to provide it before proceeding to the next level.

c. Proceed from one level of questions to another as long as you continue to get a positive response. When you do not get a positive response, you can say something like, "Thanks for sharing your thoughts on this. I'll keep you in my thoughts and prayers."

d. Based on their responses to the questions you have asked, prayerfully determine an appropriate "next step" for them. No matter how they answer the questions you ask, there is always some appropriate "next step."

e. After you ask a question, wait for an answer. Do not be afraid of silence. Silence creates a vacuum. If you do not break it the other person will. They will likely answer your question directly or indirectly.

f. It may be that the person does not have an answer at that time, but the very fact that they have heard the question is like a seed being planted. They will think about it. God will bring it to their mind at the appropriate times.

2. Progressive Levels of Questions:

After you have presented the Bible truth and your own testimony regarding the Bible's prescription for health, the following list of progressively escalating questions will help you determine the level of decision a person is ready to make. When multiple options are provided, they will be indicated by numbers. (They are not progressive.) Pray that the Holy Spirit will guide you in determining the most appropriate option, which may be different than those suggested. And remember, regardless of what the immediate results appear to be, the Holy Spirit will always use such conversations to His advantage to reach hearts for eternity. Trust in God and He will ensure that your faithful efforts bear fruit.

	Question(s) for a Christian	Question(s) for a Non-Christian
Level 1: Understanding Grasp of the truth about the Bible's health plan (includes the biblical truth and your personal testimony related to it)	1. "Does what I've shared about the Bible's teaching on health make sense to you?" 2. "Can you see how my understanding of the Bible's health plan gives me a blueprint for healthy living?" 3. "As someone like you, who has accepted Jesus as Lord of my life and believes my body is the temple of the Holy Spirit, can you see why I'm excited about the Bible's health plan?" 4. "Do you have any questions about what the Bible teaches about healthy living?"	1. "Does what I've shared about the Bible's teaching on health make sense to you?" 2. "Can you see how my understanding of the Bible's health plan gives me a blueprint for healthy living?" 3. "Can you see why I'm excited about the Bible's health plan?" 4. "Do you have any questions about what the Bible teaches about healthy living?"

	Question(s) for a Christian	Question(s) for a Non-Christian
Level 2: Desire Sense of personal need for the benefit that the Bible's health plan could add to their life	1. "Can you see how someone who clearly understands what the Bible teaches about healthy living would have an advantage?" (e.g., how many broken homes might possibly have remained intact, or motorists' lives might have been saved, if the eleven million alcoholics in the United States had never touched alcohol?) 2. "Is there anything about the Adventists' understanding of the Bible's prescription for good health that you think you could benefit from?"	1. "When you hear about these teachings of the Bible relative to healthy living, can you identify any specific teaching that you think could be beneficial to you?" 2. "Can you see that if everyone followed the Bible's prescription for healthy living there would be a lot less disease and suffering in the world today?" 3. "The revelation that my body is the temple of God is such a lofty idea to me. Can you understand why that motivates me to want to live the healthiest life possible, and to want to follow the Bible's plan for healthy living?" 4. "Wouldn't it be great to be free from smoking (or any other perceived physical addiction)?" Before asking that question, you have to know the person well enough so that they know you are not criticizing them for their habit, but rather want the very best for them.

	Question(s) for a Christian	Question(s) for a Non-Christian
Level 3: Conviction How strongly they feel it is important to act on the issues related to the Bible's health plan	1. "Do you ever wish you lived a healthier lifestyle than you sometimes do?" 2. "If you could make just one change to align yourself with the Bible's health plan as you understand it, what would it be?"	1. "If you knew you couldn't fail, and were invited to choose one change you'd like to make to have a healthier lifestyle, what would it be?" If their desired change is in the direction of a biblical health principle (eating healthier, rest, trust in God, etc.), affirm them in their choice and assure them that God would be excited to help them and will help them if they ask. You may also want to offer your support (while not being pushy), or ask them if there might be anything you could do to be a support to them on that point. You can always assure them of your prayers.

	Question(s) for a Christian	Question(s) for a Non-Christian
Next Step Appropriate follow-up action they, or you, might take in support of their spiritual journey, based on your perception of their readiness to accept it	1. "Would you be interested in studying more about health principles advocated in the Bible? I have a great book I could lend you." (Check your local ABC for a recent book on healthy living, integrating Scripture as well as scientific information.) 2. "I'm going to a nutrition class. It'd be fun if you would go with me; we could do it together." 3. "Would you be interested in studying more about this subject? I have a great Bible study on this subject that we could go through together." 4. "Would you be interested in coming over to my house some evening for some healthy snacks and to watch a really good video that explains this further?" (For example: any evangelistic series video on the subject of health)	1. "Would you be interested in learning more about what the Bible teaches about health? I have a great book I could lend you." (Check your local ABC for a recent book on health.) 2. "I'm going to a nutrition class. It'd be fun if you would go with me; we could do it together." 3. "Would you be interested in studying together more of what the Bible teaches about good health and how to have it?" 4. "Would you be interested in coming over to my house some evening for some healthy snacks and to watch a really good video that explains this further?" (For example: any evangelistic series video on the subject of health)

3. Decision Texts Related to the Bible's Teaching on Health

a. "Dear friend, I pray that you may enjoy good health and that all may go well with you, even as your soul is getting along well." (3 John 2)

b. "I have come that they might have life, and have it to the full." (John 10:10)

c. "Is any one of you sick? He should call the elders of the church to pray over him and anoint him with oil in the name of the Lord. And the prayer offered in faith will make the sick person well; the Lord will raise him up. If he has sinned, he will be forgiven." (James 5:14–15)

D. Homework

1. **Read Preview for Session 8**: God's sandbox illustration of redemption.

2. Look for opportunities to share the **NEWSTART ®** acronym.

3. Talk with your health and temperance leader about sponsoring some type of health seminar at your church.

4. Call LifestyleMatters TM to order some attractive *Balance* magazines to put on your desk at work or share with your friends. These are great conversation starters. Visit their website to view the material: www.lifestylematters.com. Click SHOP; click *Balance* Magazine. Call: 866-624-5433 to order.

PREVIEW FOR SESSION 8: THE SANCTUARY

What Makes Seventh-day Adventism Unique and Contagious?

At the end of his excellent book, *A Search for Identity: The Development of Seventh-day Adventist Beliefs*, George Knight summarizes the uniqueness of Seventh-day Adventism that holds the secret to its vitality and contagiousness as a worldwide movement:

"Adventist history demonstrates two essential clusters of truth that define what it means to be a Seventh-day Adventist Christian.

"The first are the central pillar doctrines developed in the early years of Adventism: the seventh-day Sabbath, the Second Advent, the two-phase ministry of Christ in the heavenly sanctuary, conditional immortality, and the perpetuity of spiritual gifts (including the gift of prophecy) until the end of time....

"The second absolutely central cluster in Adventist theology consists of a number of beliefs that Adventism shares with other Christians, such as the Godhead; the divine inspiration of the Bible; the problem of sin; the life, substitutionary death, and resurrection of Jesus; and the plan of salvation....

"But the genius of Seventh-day Adventism does not lie so much in those doctrines that make it distinctive or in those beliefs that it shares with other Christians. Rather it is a combination of both sets of understandings within the framework of the Great Controversy theme found in the apocalyptic core of the book of Revelation running from Revelation 11:19 through the end of chapter 14. It is that prophetic insight that distinguishes Seventh-day Adventism from other Adventists, other sabbatarians, and all other Christians. The Great Controversy theology (first worked out by [Joseph] Bates in the mid-1840's) has led Seventh-day Adventism to see itself as a prophetic people. That understanding has driven Adventists to the far corners of the earth as they have sought to sound the messages of the three angels before the great harvest day. *When that vision is lost, Seventh-day Adventism will have lost its genius. It will have become merely another somewhat harmless denomination with some peculiar doctrines instead of being a dynamic movement of prophecy.*" (pp. 204–205)

The topics chosen for the Contagious Adventist Seminar do indeed integrate some of the great biblical themes we share with other Christians (Jesus is Lord, etc.) with the more unique doctrines of Adventists (Sabbath, State of the Dead, etc.) in a Great Controversy perspective. Interestingly, these topics were chosen, as reported earlier in the seminar, based on what the Seventh-day Adventist converts we surveyed told us most attracted them to the Adventist church (including the Adventist emphasis on health).

The Overlooked and Abused Pillar

The unique Adventist doctrine we have not discussed previously is the Adventist understanding of the sanctuary. Very few of those converts we surveyed identified the teaching about the sanctuary as an influence that attracted them to the Adventist church, perhaps because it had not been emphasized in their preparation to becoming a member of the church, or perhaps because they did not understand its significance. Yet Dr. Knight referred to "the two-phase ministry of Christ in the heavenly sanctuary" as one of the "central pillars" of Adventist teaching. And Ellen White cited the heavenly sanctuary as one of the three "landmarks" of Adventism, along with the Sabbath and the non-immortality of the soul. (*Counsel to Writers and Editors*, pp. 30–31)

The sanctuary may be the most overlooked and abused teaching of the church:

- Abused in that a few fringe groups talk about nothing else and mistakenly make it out to be the one true identifying mark of Adventism, and thus more important than any of our other beliefs.

- Overlooked in that it is inadvertently ignored by many leaders and lay members alike.

We have decided to include this session in the Contagious Adventist Seminar so that we do not make the same mistake of overlooking a pillar and landmark of Adventist identity simply because it did not rate high on our survey of what influenced people to become Seventh-day Adventists.

Spotlight on Jesus

Everything in the Old Testament sanctuary pointed to Jesus and His saving grace.

1. The sanctuary/temple/tabernacle, the physical location where God dwelt among His people during the Old Testament, represented Jesus who came and dwelt (literally "tabernacled") among us in the flesh (Exodus 25:8; John 1:14—the word "dwelling" here is the verb form of the Greek noun for "sanctuary" in Heb 8:5; 9:1; etc.).

2. The slain lambs at the Altar of Burnt Offering represented Jesus, the Lamb of God slain for our sins from the foundation of the world (John 1:29; Revelation 13:8).

3. The cleansing water of the Laver represented Jesus cleansing the believer through the work of the Holy Spirit (John 7:37–39; Titus 3:5).

4. The sanctuary Shewbread represented Jesus, the bread of life (John 6:35).

5. The sanctuary Lamp stand represented Jesus, the light of the world (John 8:12).

6. The Altar of Incense represented the sweet-smelling aroma of Jesus' sacrificial love and righteousness which are mingled with our prayers as they ascend as fragrant incense to God (Ephesians 5:2; Revelation 8:3).

7. The Atonement Cover or Mercy Seat over the Ark of the Covenant represented Jesus' atoning sacrifice for our sins (Leviticus 16:2; Romans 3:25—the terms "sacrifice of atonement" NIV & NRSV, "propitiation" NKJV, and "mercy seat" KJV & RSV, in these verses are English translations of the same Greek word, *hilastarion*).

8. The priests who officiated at the sanctuary represented Jesus, the one true "mediator between God and men" (1 Timothy 2:5).

To study the sanctuary is to study about Jesus at every turn.

Spotlight on a Saving Response to Jesus' Gift of Salvation
The sanctuary symbolically portrays how we come to Jesus and grow in Jesus.

1. The sacrifice of a goat or lamb made by the sinner at the Altar of Burnt Offering represented repentance and faith as a means of receiving God's gift of forgiveness and salvation (Leviticus 4:27–32; Acts 2:38; 16:30–33).

2. The Laver of water between the Altar of Burnt Offering and the sanctuary may be viewed as symbolizing the new birth into the kingdom of God through baptism of water (New Testament rite) and the Spirit (John 3:3–8; Titus 3:3–8).

3. The Shewbread in the sanctuary symbolized feeding on the Word of God for spiritual growth (Matthew 4:4).

4. The incense from the Altar of Incense represented our prayers ascending to God (Revelation 5:8; 8:3).

5. The light of the temple Lamp stand represented unselfish service to others through which God's love is revealed (Matthew 5:14–16).

6. The bright light which according to ancient tradition emanated from the Mercy Seat over the Ark of the Covenant represented the presence and glory of God among His people, inviting us to live for God's glory in everything that we do (Exodus 25:21–22; 1 Corinthians 10:31).

Spotlight on the Final Judgment
The Old Testament sanctuary's annual Day of Atonement was considered by the Israelites as an annual day of judgment. On that day atonement and cleansing was made for all the people and even for the sanctuary itself (Leviticus 16:29–33). Anyone who did not "afflict his soul" or "deny himself" on that day, in the sense of being repentant for sins and rededicated to God and His truths that were symbolically represented in the sanctuary, was to be "cut off from his people" (Leviticus 16:29–34; 23:26–29).

In 586 B.C., the Babylonians destroyed the sanctuary/temple in Jerusalem. Daniel was later shown in vision that after 2,300 days the sanctuary would again be cleansed, but also that the 2,300 days would reach to "the time of the end" (Daniel 8:14–17). The 2,300-day period of Daniel's vision represented 2,300 years, which began in 457 B.C. with Artaxerxes' command to restore and rebuild Jerusalem and the temple at the end of the Babylonian exile, and ended in 1844 A.D., "the time of the end" (Ezra 7:1, 8–26; Daniel 9:20–25). By 1844 A.D., however, the rebuilt earthly temple was gone, having been destroyed by the Romans in 70 A.D. This prophecy, therefore, must have in mind the heavenly sanctuary, after which the earthly sanctuary had been patterned (Exodus 25:9; Hebrews 8:5).

Thus in 1844 the final Day of Atonement and cleansing of the sanctuary began in heaven, commencing the final judgment of the world (Daniel 7:9–10). It was at this time that our world was ushered into the awesome era the Bible calls "the time of the end" (Daniel 8:17, 19). At this time also the first angel's message of Revelation 14 became particularly applicable: "Fear God and give him glory, because the hour of his judgment has come" (v. 7).

Before Jesus returns, the investigative phase of the final judgment, symbolized by the Old Testament sanctuary's Day of Atonement, will have been completed. In this investigative phase the final rewards of the saved and unsaved will be determined. Jesus affirmed this by declaring: "Behold, I am coming soon! My reward is with me, and I will give to everyone according to what he has done" (Revelation 22:12). We live in the time when that investigative phase of the final judgment is proceeding in heaven. At its conclusion, Jesus will return with His rewards!

Daniel's vision prophesied that an enemy power would attack the truths of the sanctuary and throw them to the ground (Daniel 8:9–12). Is it any wonder that Satan hates the sanctuary and the awesome truths it represents? The sanctuary focuses on Jesus, symbolically portrays how we come to Jesus and grow in Jesus, and alerts us to the awesome reality that we do indeed live in "the time of the end" with Jesus soon to return.

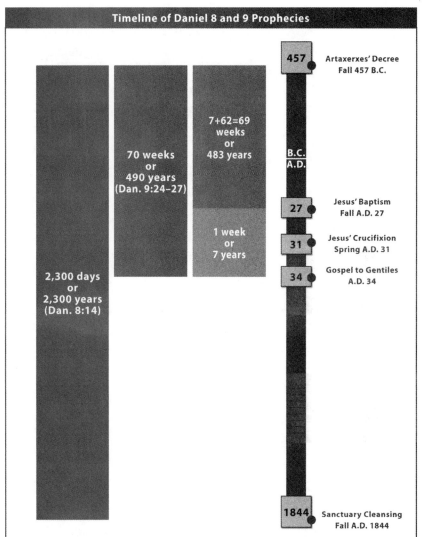

Timeline of Daniel 8 and 9 Prophecies

457 — Artaxerxes' Decree Fall 457 B.C.

7+62=69 weeks or 483 years

70 weeks or 490 years (Dan. 9:24–27)

B.C. / A.D.

27 — Jesus' Baptism Fall A.D. 27

1 week or 7 years

31 — Jesus' Crucifixion Spring A.D. 31

34 — Gospel to Gentiles A.D. 34

2,300 days or 2,300 years (Dan. 8:14)

1844 — Sanctuary Cleansing Fall A.D. 1844

457 B.C. Beginning of the 70 weeks (490 years). Marked by the command to restore and rebuild Jerusalem (9:25) issued by the Persian king Artaxerxes I in the seventh year of his reign (Ezra 7:11–26).

A.D. 27. End of the 69 weeks (483 years) predicted for the coming of Messiah the Prince (Dan. 9:25) and beginning of the last week. Fulfilled in the fifteenth year of the reign of Tiberius Caesar when Jesus was baptized and began His ministry (Luke 3:1, 21).

A.D. 31. Middle of the last week (Dan. 9:27) of the 70 weeks (490 years). After 3 1/2 years of earthly ministry, the death of Christ confirmed a covenant for the benefit of all.

A.D. 34. End of the 70 weeks (490 years). Marked by the martyrdom of Stephen and the related persecution that scattered Christians from Judea, and thus spread the gospel to the Gentiles.

A.D. 1844. End of the 2,300 days (2,300 years). Marked the beginning of the cleansing of the heavenly sanctuary and the end-time work of judgment.

Session 8

The Sanctuary: God's Illustration of Redemption

In this session we will:

1. Explore the biblical doctrine of the sanctuary.

2. Explore practical applications of the sanctuary truth for our lives today.

3. Learn how to draw and explain the sanctuary diagram.

4. Learn the skills needed to share this subject as a Contagious Adventist.

5. Learn how to ask for a decision related to the Sanctuary.

A. Relevance of the Biblical Truth of the Sanctuary for Today

1. An age-old issue resolved in the sanctuary.

    a. The author of Psalm 73 wrestled with a problem—Why do the ungodly prosper while devout believers have so many problems?

    b. "When I tried to understand all this, it was oppressive to me," he writes, "till I entered the _____ of God; then I understood their final destiny." (vv. 16–17)

    c. There was something about the meaning and symbolism and teaching of the sanctuary that reaffirmed his faith.

        1) The sanctuary taught him that God had made_____ by His grace for every sinner to be _____ to God and _____ to eternal life.

        2) The sanctuary pointed out _____ _____ the sinner could_____ that gracious gift of cleansing and eternal life from God.

        3) The sanctuary showed the _____ a believer could take to continue to _____ in their relationship to God so that their life would be a more effective _____ that would _____ _____ to God and eternal life.

        4) The annual ritual of the _____ _____ _____taught that all of life on this earth is preparation to stand before God in the _____ _____ of all humankind.

        And no matter how prosperous or famous one may become

in this life, if they do not accept God's provision for salvation and grow in their relationship with God, they will ultimately lose everything, including eternity.

5) The truth taught in the sanctuary affirmed that faith in God, and living a life to_____ God and _____ others is the most meaningful and hopeful life possible on this earth, even if your life may have its trials.

6) This assurance gave the perplexed and despairing author of Psalm 73 renewed _____ and _____.

7) Everything necessary for salvation was taught and represented through the _____.

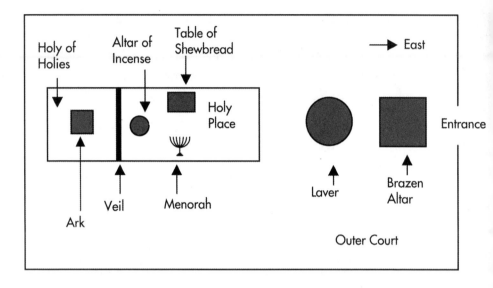

d. The Symbolism of the Temple for the Plan of Salvation

Physical Structure/Symbols	Jesus	Our Response to Jesus
Sanctuary/Temple/ Tabernacle Exodus 25:8	"Dwelt (tabernacled) among us" John 1:14	Our bodies are "the temple of God" 1 Corinthians 6:19
1. Altar of Burnt Offering— Lamb sacrifice Exodus 27:1–8 Leviticus 4:27-32	The "Lamb of God" slain for our sins Isaiah 53:4–12 John 1:29	Repentance and faith in the atoning sacrifice of Jesus Acts 2:38; 16:30–33
2. Laver—Cleansing water Exodus 30:17–21	The Water of Life John 4:13–14	New birth—NT baptism John 3:3–8 Titus 3:3–8
3. Table for "Bread of the Presence" Exodus 25:23–30	The "Bread of Life" John 6:35	Study the Word of God Matthew 4:4
4. Lamp stand—Lamps Exodus 25:31–37	The "Light of the world" John 8:12	Good works—Loving service to others Matthew 5:14–16
5. Altar of Incense Exodus 30:1–8	"A fragrant offering and sacrifice to God" Ephesians 5:2	Prayer Revelation 5:8; 8:3
6. Ark of the Covenant Exodus 25:10–15 a. Atonement Cover— Mercy Seat—The divine presence Exodus 25:17–22 Leviticus 16:2 b. Testimony—Ten Commandments Exodus 25:16, 21–22	a. "Sacrifice of atone- ment," "propitiation," "mercy seat" Romans 3:25 1 John 2:2 b. "The righteousness of the law" revealed in His character Romans 3:21–22	a. Living in Jesus' pres- ence—Living to glorify God John 15:4–5 1 Corinthians 10:31 b. God's law written in the heart and lived out in the life Romans 8:4 Hebrews 8:10

ACTIVITY (1): Draw and explain the sanctuary diagram.

1. Diagram

2. The biblical doctrine of the sanctuary has extreme importance to the Seventh-day Adventist movement.

   a. The followers of _____ _____interpreted "the cleansing of the sanctuary" (KJV) prophesied in Daniel 8:14 to mean that Jesus' _____ _____ would occur on October 22, 1844, at the end of the 2,300 days/years.

   b. When Jesus did not come when they expected, God gave a relatively unknown Adventist believer, Hiram Edson, an insight that provided an explanation.

   Based on texts from Daniel 7, Hebrews 8–9, and Revelation 10–11, he came to understand that the sanctuary God would cleanse in 1844 was _____ the _____, but the sanctuary in _____.

   c. Early Adventist believers found their great disappointment in 1844 reflected in Revelation 10.

   In that chapter an angelic representative of Jesus told John to eat a little book which would be _____ in his mouth but _____ in his stomach (v. 10).

   This small band of Millerites could readily identify with John's experience.

     1) They had eaten, or studied thoroughly, the prophecies of the little book of Daniel and found them to be sweet in their mouth as they proclaimed them with joy. It was **sweet** because they believed that Daniel 8:14–17 prophesied that Jesus would return on October 22, 1844, cleanse the earth, and take them to heaven with Him.

     2) But when Jesus did not come as they expected, their experience turned very **bitter.**

     Revelation 10 seemed to assure them that God had anticipated their bitter disappointment and had provided a special message of affirmation that He was still with them and leading them.

156 | Contagious Adventist

d. These believers found in the very next verse that God still had a mission for them:

"Thou must _____ _____ before many peoples, and nations, and tongues, and kings" (Revelation 10:11, KJV).

e. In the next chapter, Revelation 11, they found confirmation that the temple that had begun to be cleansed in 1844 was not the earth after all.

(They had mistakenly believed that the sanctuary or temple referred to in Daniel 8:14 was the earth, and that the cleansing Daniel prophesied about would be the fire that would cleanse the earth at the Second Coming of Jesus.)

What they found was that it was not the earth, but rather the temple in heaven which would begin to be cleansed in 1844. Revelation 11:19 says,

"Then God's temple _____ _____ was opened, and within his temple was seen the ark of his covenant."

That was the ark in the most holy place which contained the Ten Commandments and which John now saw in the temple in heaven.

f. These believers then compared Daniel 8:14 with Leviticus 16's description of the cleansing of the Old Testament sanctuary on the annual Day of Atonement.

The Israelites considered the

Day of Atonement as the _____ judgment of their

_____.

This led our **early pioneers** to conclude that:

The cleansing of the sanctuary in heaven, beginning in 1844, was the beginning of the _____ judgment of the

_____.

| Israelites | Annual Day of Atonement | Judgment | Nation |
| Early Pioneers | Final Day of Atonement began in 1844 | Judgment | World |

g. In Revelation 11:1 they discovered this command: "Go and measure the temple of God and the altar, and count the worshipers there."

So again, there definitely seemed to be something about the sanctuary that God wanted them to study and understand.

h. In Revelation 14:6–12 they rediscovered the three angels' messages which God said were to be proclaimed just

_____ ____ _____ _____ _____ of

Jesus described in the very next verses (14–16).

i. So from their study of Revelation 10–14 the early Adventist pioneers concluded the following:

1) God had affirmed the _____ they had passed through in the great disappointment (10:10),

2) God was directing their attention to His _____ _____ _____and to the truths taught there (11:1, 19),

3) God had guided them to the _____ _____ _____ which He wanted them to carry to the final generation (14:6–12), and

4) God had assigned them a mission to _____ _____ _____ with the whole world (10:11).

3. So, how should the Bible's teaching of the sanctuary and of the final judgment of the world beginning in 1844 affect our lives in a practical way today?

a. The message of the sanctuary is that we are saved by Jesus alone.

Jesus is our all-sufficient High Priest and mediator with God in the heavenly sanctuary (1 Timothy 2:5; Hebrews 7:23–26; 9:11).

b. God calls us to be contagious bearers and sharers of the everlasting gospel, as taught with simplicity and clarity in the symbolism of the sanctuary (Revelation 14:6–7).

c. We know that since 1844 we live at "the time of the end," the time when the heavenly sanctuary is being cleansed and judgment is proceeding in heaven (Daniel 8:14, 17, 19).

d. We live in a time of great accountability.

The final judgment of the world is taking place in heaven now.

Remembering that the final judgment is proceeding in heaven right now helps provide an important perspective on life and encourages us to focus on those things that matter most and are of eternal consequence and value (Acts 17:30–31).

e. God wants the biblical teaching of the judgment to be revived in an age when it seems largely ignored by the world and even by many churches today. Mining this great biblical theme reveals that:

1) The final judgment is not about God arbitrarily assigning some to eternal life and others to eternal damnation based on a predetermined decree made by Him before we were even born. It is about God's final acceptance of our ultimate response to His many efforts to save us.

Whether we accept or reject the salvation God offers us will be demonstrated by the public and secret actions of our everyday lives (Ecclesiastes 12:13–14).

2) The final judgment is about God defending His children against Satan's accusations that they are unworthy of eternal life (Zechariah 3:1–7).

3) The final judgment is ultimately about the character of God.

4) The final judgment is about God's children defending Him against the accusations falsely and unfairly made against Him by His archenemy.

f. Knowing the sacredness of the times in which we live is an appeal to live every aspect of our lives to the glory of God (1 Corinthians 10:31).

 VIDEO

B. Testimonies

1. Teri

I used to think that the Bible was so confusing. This church said the Bible meant one thing and another said it meant another. I shared my frustration with my friend, Jena, at work. I didn't realize at the time that Jena was a Seventh-day Adventist. She told me that what simplified the Bible and the plan of salvation for her was an illustration God used throughout the Old Testament. It was kind of like a big sandbox illustration God had His people set up in the desert to start with. Then when they built Jerusalem, He had them put it right in the middle of the city. Jena definitely had my attention, and I wanted to know more. She sketched out the layout of the Old Testament sanctuary and explained to me how every part of it pointed to Jesus as our Savior. Then she showed me how each piece of furniture, and the sacrifice ritual, showed me how I could accept Jesus and grow closer to Him. It was so simple. I've never lost that perspective and have shared it many times with friends who are as confused over the Bible as I used to be.

2. Les

My wife and I went through a Bible study series with a Seventh-day Adventist friend. All the subjects we studied seemed to us to be Bible truth. But at the end of the series we still did not feel compelled to leave the church we were worshipping in and become Seventh-day Adventists. Then our friend brought a video presentation to our home about the 2,300 day prophecy in Daniel. At the end of that study my wife and I both had the same impression—we need to make a decision and become Adventists. In spite of the fact that we had had other studies on the nearness of Jesus' return, there was something about that particular study on the 2,300 days that made it more real for us. We had never heard anything like that before, and were convinced it was true and that we needed to be sharing these Bible truths with our own friends and family. Since that study that night we have had a sense of the nearness of Jesus' coming and the importance of coming out of Babylon that we had never had before.

3. Peter

I use to believe that everyone was predestined from birth to either be saved or lost. I never really questioned this belief that was taught to me in the church I grew up in. But a friend invited me to a series of evangelistic meetings, and I heard a presentation for the first time about the final judgment that began in 1844. It made so much sense. I remembered having read texts about the judgment before. But it had never occurred to me that if God had already predestined everyone from birth to either be saved or lost, and there was nothing anyone could do to change their predetermined destiny, then what need would there be for a final judgment? Learning that God has a set time for judging the world meant to me that people really do have a choice in the matter. That was a pivotal insight that led me to see and accept God and missions in a whole new light. It's my goal in life now to live by God's grace in such a way every day that my life will be an influence to lead others to choose God and eternal life.

4. Angie

I grew up an Adventist. When I first heard that the final judgment of the world began in 1844, I used to be afraid that my name might come up before God at a time when I wasn't acceptable to Him or was committing a sin, and as a result I would be lost. That fear disappeared as I learned more about God's grace and the gospel. Once I accepted Jesus and put my faith in Him, I belonged to God and Jesus would be my representative whenever my name would come up in the judgment. I've grown to love this Bible truth of the investigative judgment. It says so much about God that He would take the time to allow the angels and other inhabitants of the universe to see all the evidence that all those He saves did indeed choose Jesus as their Savior and Lord. God allows Satan to make his accusations, and then shows the evidence that I have truly believed, and that His grace has made me a new creation. That Bible teaching has given me such wonderful respect and love for God. I want everyone to know how wonderful He is and choose to be with Him forever.

5. Devon

Growing up as an Adventist I was taught about 1844, but I really didn't understand it. It was just a confusing math thing to me. I remember that it had something to do with the judgment, but I really didn't have things like the judgment on my mind at the time. In my mid 20's I came across some literature written by former Adventists accusing Adventists of having an un-Christian understanding of Daniel 8:14 which could not be supported by careful Bible study. That stuck with me and became one of the reasons why I left the church. I went searching for a new church home and eventually ended up in a vibrant congregation that just taught the Bible. But I never completely satisfied myself that the Sabbath of the fourth commandment wasn't still part of God's plan for us today. Eventually I started asking about my new congregation's views on the prophecies. They were even more confusing to me than the Adventist explanations had been. That was an eye-opener for me. I still don't have all my questions answered about Daniel 8:14 and 1844, but once I studied it out on my own I discovered that the Adventist explanation that the final judgment began in heaven at that time, ushering the world into its final days, made more sense to me than anything else I came across. Eventually, the other Adventist teachings did also. That was part of a seven-year process the Holy Spirit took me through in leading me back to the Adventist faith with a new conviction and experience with Jesus. I'm convinced now that Jesus is coming soon.

C. Starting Conversations

1. If someone you are talking to says the Bible is confusing to them because churches all have different interpretations, you could say something like: "I can understand your point of view. Did you ever play in a sandbox when you were a child? I did. My sandbox toys were very simple compared to a lot of toys kids play with today. Well, I've found a sandbox kind of illustration that God gave in the Bible that shows in a simple way how we can connect with God and have eternal life. I'd be happy to share that with you sometime if you're interested."

2. If you hear someone refer in jesting or in a derogatory way to the idea of judgment, this would be an opportunity for you to say something to raise curiosity. Sometimes someone will say that they don't go to church because all churches do is make people feel guilty by telling them they will have to stand before God someday in judgment. When you hear these kinds of statements, you could say something like: "I can understand and appreciate what you're saying. But I learned about a prophecy in the Bible that has changed my whole understanding about what the Bible teaches about the judgment. I'd be glad to share that with you sometime if you're interested."

3. If anyone asks you if you believe in predestination, or if you hear someone advocating the teaching of predestination, you could very gently say something like: "That's a good question, a lot of people believe that. I've found a prophecy in the Bible that's really helped me with that. I'd be happy to discuss that with you sometime if you're interested."

4. "I've just been studying about the sanctuary and the judgment. I'm learning some amazing things."

5. If it is election time you could talk about the politicians and how their characters are under a microscope. God's character is on the line. That is one reason why there is a judgment...

6. When eating bread with some friends you could say, "I've been studying about the bread in the sanctuary...."

7. [This is for women] When you and your friends are in the ladies' room checking out your faces in the mirror, you can make a comment, "I wonder what it was like to just have brass as a mirror. I read in the Old Testament where the women contributed their brass mirrors to make the bronze basin at the entrance of the sanctuary."

D. Asking for a Decision

1. Guidelines for asking for decisions:

a. Use a series of questions to determine the level of decision a person is ready to make.

b. Always begin with general questions to determine their understanding of the subject and if they need further information. If more is needed, make arrangements to provide it before proceeding to the next level.

c. Proceed from one level of questions to another as long as you continue to get a positive response. When you do not get a positive response, you can say something like, "Thanks for sharing your thoughts on this. I'll keep you in my thoughts and prayers."

d. Based on their responses to the questions you have asked, prayerfully determine an appropriate "next step" for them. No matter how they answer the questions you ask, there is always some appropriate "next step."

e. After you ask a question, wait for an answer. Do not be afraid of silence. Silence creates a vacuum. If you do not break it the other person will. They will likely answer your question directly or indirectly.

f. It may be that the person does not have an answer at that time, but the very fact that they have heard the question is like a seed being planted. They will think about it. God will bring it to their mind at the appropriate times.

2. Progressive Levels of Questions:

The following grid suggests three progressively escalating levels of questions. These questions would be appropriate to ask after you have shared the Bible truth and your own personal testimony about the sanctuary. When multiple options are provided, they will be indicated by numbers. (They are not progressive.) Pray that the Holy Spirit will guide you in determining the most appropriate option, which may be different than those suggested.

	Question(s) for a Christian	Question(s) for a Non-Christian
Level 1: Understanding Grasp of the truth about the sanctuary and the final judgment (includes the biblical truth and your personal testimony related to it)	1. "Does what I've shared about the sanctuary (and/or the final judgment) make sense to you?" 2. "Do you have any questions about how I understand what the Bible teaches about the sanctuary (and/or the final judgment)?"	1. "Can you see how the Bible teaching about the sanctuary shows how important Jesus is to a Christian?" 2. "Can you see why I believe it's so important today to understand the Bible teaching about the sanctuary?"
Level 2: Desire Sense of personal need for the benefit that the truth about the sanctuary (and/or the final judgment) could add to their life	1. "Can you see how the Bible teaching about the sanctuary helps me appreciate and love Jesus more?" 2. "Can you see how the teaching of the investigative judgment helps us realize that we really do live at the time of the end and can look forward to Jesus' soon return?"	1. "Can you see how the Bible teaching about the sanctuary makes me so excited about Jesus and why He means so much to me?" 2. "Can you see how the sanctuary illustrates how a person can connect with God and have a relationship with God?"

	Question(s) for a Christian	Question(s) for a Non-Christian
Level 3: Conviction How strongly they feel it is important to act on truth about the sanctuary (and/or the final judgment)	1. "Can you see how learning more about the sanctuary might help you explain the gospel to some of your friends?" 2. "Can you see how this subject of the final judgment that is already taking place in heaven might help some people realize that they need to come to God before it is too late?"	1. "Would you be interested in learning more about this Jesus who is represented all through the symbolism of the sanctuary?" 2. "Does the Bible teaching that the final judgment is already taking place in heaven help you grasp why connecting with God is such an urgent matter today?"
Next Step Appropriate follow-up action they, or you, might take in support of their spiritual journey, based on your perception of their readiness to accept it	1. "Would you be interested in learning more about this subject? I have a great book I could lend you." (For example: *Who's Afraid of the Judgment?* by Roy Gane) 2. "Would you be interested in coming over to my house some evening for some refreshments and to watch a really good video that explains this further?" (For example: any video on the sanctuary or the judgment from an evangelistic series)	1. "Would you be interested in learning more about this subject? I have a great book I could lend you." (For example: *Who's Afraid of the Judgment?* by Roy Gane) 2. "Would you be interested in coming over to my house some evening for some refreshments and to watch a really good video that explains this further?" (For example: any video on the sanctuary or the judgment from an evangelistic series)

E. Homework

1. **Read preview for Session 9,** the Seventh-day Adventist Movement.

2. Practice drawing the timeline of the 2,300-day prophecy.

3. Convince someone to let you explain the prophecy to them as part of your homework.

4. Pray that the Holy Spirit will use you this week to make an eternal difference in someone's life.

Great words of hope from *Testimonies*, Volume 5, p. 474

"The people of God have been in many respects very faulty. Satan has an accurate knowledge of the sins which he has tempted them to commit, and he presents these in the most exaggerated light, declaring: 'Will God banish me and my angels from His presence, and yet reward those who have been guilty of the same sins? Thou canst not do this, O Lord, in justice. Thy throne will not stand in righteousness and judgment. Justice demands that sentence be pronounced against them.'

"But while the followers of Christ have sinned, they have not given themselves to the control of evil. They have put away their sins, and have sought the Lord in humility and contrition, and the divine Advocate pleads in their behalf. He who has been most abused by their ingratitude, who knows their sin, and also their repentance, declares: '"'The Lord rebuke thee, O Satan.' I gave My life for these souls. They are graven upon the palms of My hands.'"

PREVIEW FOR SESSION 9:
THE SEVENTH-DAY ADVENTIST MOVEMENT

Everyone loves a great success-against-the-odds story—Bill Gates and his friends started Microsoft in a garage. Larry Page and Sergery Brin launched Google from their dorm rooms at Stanford. Great things often spring from small beginnings.

That is true of the Seventh-day Adventist movement as well.

Contagious Adventists—the Amazing Story

On October 22, 1844, small groups of Bible students, feeling devastated that Jesus had not returned the day before as they had expected, huddled in prayer. They earnestly sought God's guidance to better understand the Scriptures and to know where to go from there. God answered their prayers. Something was born in the hearts of that small community of praying believers that grew step by step into what we know today as the Seventh-day Adventist Church.

Consider this:

The Adventist Church was officially organized in 1863 with 3,500 members out of a global population of one billion (one Adventist for every three million people). Now, based on the latest statistics available as of this writing, June 30, 2012, the Adventist church worldwide:

1. Has 17,594,723 million baptized members and 19,368,905 million Sabbath School members out of a global population of 7 billion (one Adventist for every 397 people).[2]

2. Has an organized work in 209 of the 232 countries recognized by the United Nations.

3. Operates 173 hospitals and sanitariums, and 432 medical clinics and dispensaries.

---

2. Based on the growth rate for the past 20 years, membership should be 26 million by 2016, one Adventist for every 280 people.

4. Operates the largest Protestant educational system—7,806 schools (including 80 colleges and universities), with a combined student enrollment of 1,668,754. (12-31-10)

5. Operates one of the most expansive publishing programs of any Christian Church—63 publishing houses printing in 377 languages.

6. Receives more contributions annually per capita than any Christian Church,[3] enabling it to accomplish the amazing things mentioned above. (Tithe and offerings as of December 2010: $2,900,945,610)

7. Operates the Adventist Development and Relief Agency (ADRA)— one of the most respected and expansive humanitarian organizations in the world—in 125 countries, making contributions worth $59.8 million in 2011, to relieve suffering in the world.

From a small prayer group to a worldwide, contagious movement making a global impact! Quite a story indeed! Better yet, you're part of the story!

Small in Size, Big in Impact

Most Adventist churches around the world are quite small—fewer than 100 members. (This is also true for other Christian churches.) As a member of a small Adventist church, you may be unaware of the impact that your church makes on the world. But when a small church teams up with thousands of other churches like their own, the global impact can be enormous.

The Adventist Church is organized so that the larger churches help support smaller ones. That's why several small churches in a district can have a full-time pastor whose support comes in part from the tithe of larger churches. Adventist churches in wealthier countries help support

---

3. Statistics available as of this writing: $165 per baptized member worldwide, $1,200 per baptized member in North America; compared to $621 average per capita contribution of 11 North American denominations, including Southern Baptist Convention, United Church of Christ, Presbyterian Church U.S.A., Evangelical Lutheran Church in America and Seventh-day Adventists (information reported by non-denominational Empty Tomb, Inc.).

those in poorer ones. And even small churches support foreign missions through their offerings. This makes it possible for the Adventist Church to operate hospitals and schools and an expansive mission work in some very poor countries.

Whatever the size of your local Adventist church, you are part of an exciting worldwide movement that is making a global impact. As an Adventist, you are a member of a worldwide family working together with other brothers and sisters you have never met to build up and edify the kingdom of God on earth.

Satan would like to keep this information hidden. He would like you to think that your local church is so small, so weak, or so ineffective that it can't possibly make a difference in God's plan to save the world. He would like you to believe that your contribution and ministry in your local church doesn't count for much in the great controversy between Christ and Satan. Nothing could be farther from the truth.

It's true that the Adventist Church is still relatively small in numbers compared to the world's population of six billion people. But Jesus said His church is like leaven or yeast (Matthew 13:33). If you've ever baked bread, you know that just a little yeast makes an entire batch of dough rise. The church is like that. Your church may be small in comparison to the population of your community, but its influence can be significant.

There's no basis for pride here. But we should be thankful for what God is doing through our church. And our gratitude should lead us to a renewed sense of responsibility and dedication to making our own unique contribution to the awesome things God is doing in the world through our church.

The Contagious Adventist Priority One

In our previous sessions we've reviewed some wonderful, biblical reasons to be a contagious Adventist. But the Adventist Church is more than a depository for *correct doctrine*, as important as that is. It's also a *worldwide, contagious movement* dedicated to uplifting people physically, mentally, socially, and spiritually. "To take people right where they are, whatever their position or condition, and help them in every way possible—this is gospel ministry" (*Testimonies for the Church*, vol. 6, 301).

Underlying every ministry of the church is the commission Jesus gave— "Go and make disciples of all nations, baptizing them in the name of the Father and of the Son and of the Holy Spirit, and teaching them to obey everything I have commanded you" (Matthew 28:19–20). When you engage in ministry through your church, you walk with Jesus, for in His very next breath He promised those who contribute in various ways to carrying out His commission, "And surely I am with you always, to the very end of the age" (Matthew 28:20).

Every ministry of the church has an eye toward that "very end of the age" when, in Jesus' words, "I will come back and take you to be with me that you also may be where I am," and the great controversy will be ended (John 14:3).

Thank you for the contribution you are making to this exciting movement. If you aren't engaged yet, this is your official invitation to become a Contagious Adventist and join the adventure!

Session 9

The Seventh-day Adventist Movement

In this session we will:

1. Tap into our heritage and see modern evidences of God's leading in the Adventist movement.

2. Learn Seven Habits of Highly Contagious Adventists.

3. Write a personal Contagious Adventist Mission Statement.

The Seventh-day Adventist Movement

A. The Seven Habits of Highly Contagious Adventists

God raised up the Seventh-day Adventist Church in the mid nineteenth century and implanted in it His own passion for mission and evangelism. He called Adventists to be prepared, and to help others prepare, for the imminent return of Jesus. This is what makes us not just Adventists, but *Contagious Adventists.* Jesus has given us hope in His soon return. And He has called us to help others prepare for His coming.

Jesus commissioned the church to "make disciples of all nations... teaching them to obey everything I have commanded you" (Matthew 28:19–20). Every Adventist Christian is commissioned to play some role in the fulfillment of this mission. As awesome as it seems, the Bible says that as we "live holy and godly lives" and "look forward to" Jesus' return, we can actually "speed its coming" (2 Peter 3:11–12). Talk about a reason to be contagious!

God led the Seventh-day Adventist Church from its inception to focus on seven facets of ministry, patterned after the ministry of Jesus. We might think of them as the Seven Habits of Highly Contagious Adventists. All seven habits have a personal application that we can each practice. The seven habits also represent important branches of church ministry through which God has grown a small group of 3,500 Adventists in 1863 to 17.6 million in 2012.[4]

In this lesson we will identify the Seven Habits of Highly Contagious Adventists and consider the potential they have for impacting ourselves, those around us, and the world.

1. Ellen White

Besides the influence of the Scriptures themselves and the direct leadings of the Holy Spirit in many lives, perhaps no single influence has been so profoundly responsible for the expansion and growth of the Seventh-day Adventist Church as the sanctified vision, inspired writings, and personal example of Ellen G. White.

---

4. Statistics can be updated at www.adventiststatistics.org.

She was raised as a Methodist. She was only a teenager in the 1840s when she joined the small community of praying Bible students through whom God raised up the Seventh-day Adventist movement.

God called Ellen White to a role that the Seventh-day Adventist Church recognizes as a prophetic gift from God. It is an amazing story. She received only a few years of formal education, yet during her 70-year ministry she was enabled by the Holy Spirit to author more than 5,000 articles, over 200 hundred tracts, and 40 books. These publications with over 50,000 extant manuscript pages she wrote have yielded more than 100 books. Many of her books have been translated from English into other languages. She may well be the most translated woman author in the history of literature and the most translated American author of either gender. *Steps to Christ*, her masterpiece on how to become a thriving Christian, has been translated into more than 165 languages. Her writings are rooted in Scripture and Christ-centered throughout. Those who read her writings are instilled with a love for Jesus, a love for His word, and a passion for the salvation of others.

See Appendix A, Session 9, for the results of a church growth survey that compared readers and non-readers of Ellen White. The graph shows how each group responded to questions related to 19 areas of spiritual life. "In the church growth survey, on *every single item* that deals with personal attitudes or practices, the member who regularly studies Ellen White's books tends to rate higher than does the member who reads them occasionally or never."

The graph depicts the results of research done on over 8,000 Seventh-day Adventists in North America.[5]

The unique vision and encouragement God gave to the church through the ministry of Ellen White led the church to focus on six major areas of ministry that are patterned after the ministry of Christ. These six ministries make up the other 6 habits of highly contagious Adventists:

a. World Evangelization

b. Publishing Ministry

c. Medical Ministry

d. Christian Education

e. Community Service

f. Christian Stewardship

A passion for missions grows out of the Seventh-day Adventist theological framework and is enhanced by the influence of Ellen White's writings and ministry..

When you read the writings of Ellen White and share them with others (especially books like *Steps to Christ*, *The Desire of Ages*, *Great Controversy*, *Christ's Object Lessons*, and *Thoughts From the Mount of Blessing*) you avail yourself and others of this divine gift and you *practice the first habit of highly contagious Adventists.*

2. World Evangelization

Adventist foreign missions began with great sacrifice. In 1874 the church sent John Nevins Andrews, a former General Conference

---

5. Roger L. Dudley, Des Cummings, Jr., "Who Reads Ellen White?" *Ministry,* October, 1982, pp. 10–12. These researchers add: "Seldom does a research study find the evidence so heavily weighted toward one conclusion. In the church growth survey, on *every single item* that deals with personal attitudes or practices, the member who regularly studies Ellen White's books tends to rate higher than does the member who reads them occasionally or never....*On no item do nonreaders rate higher than readers.*" (Emphasis in original.)

president and editor of the Review and Herald, as its first officially sponsored foreign missionary. He left for Europe as a single parent, accompanied by his two children, Charles and Mary. His wife had died two years earlier. The missionary family wrote, translated, published, and distributed the *Signs of the Times* magazine for European audiences. After four years in Europe, Mary died of tuberculosis. Although this was a terrible blow to Andrews, he would not be deterred. He continued his missionary work in Europe until his own death from tuberculosis five years later. Andrews was a godly biblical scholar and author who spent much time in prayer. He had memorized the New Testament and large portions of the Old Testament. When Battle Creek College, the church's first institution of higher education, moved to Berrien Springs, Michigan, it became Emmanuel Missionary College. In 1960 it was renamed Andrews University in his honor—to be a University that would continue to prepare students to sacrificially serve God around the world.

Based on the gospel commission Jesus gave His church in Matthew 28:19–20, world evangelization continues to be priority one of the Seventh-day Adventist Church. The American Bible Society once published a chart listing the worldwide established missions of 63 of the largest Protestant denominations. The five highest in reverse order were:

5) Southern Baptist Convention – 63 countries

4) Churches of God – 69 countries

3) Assemblies of God – 78 countries

2) Churches of God (Cleveland) – 80 countries

1) Seventh-day Adventists - 178 countries

These statistics don't prove that Seventh-day Adventists love God more than others do, but they do demonstrate the high level of commitment we have to world evangelization.

The Seventh-day Adventist Church is intentional about global mission. Through radio and television, global satellite evangelism, student mission projects, local church evangelistic meetings, Bible studies, and personal contacts, Seventh-day Adventists continue to spread the gospel of Christ around the world. The church that began as a small group in one nation has grown into a world church. Today 94% of its 17.6 million members live outside the United States.

As you use the skills you have gained in this course, *you practice Habit Two of Highly Contagious Adventists.* Every time you share your faith, you contribute to world evangelization and the growth of the kingdom of God on earth. And everyone you influence for God's kingdom becomes another link in the chain that God will use to reach more and more people until Jesus comes.

3. Publishing Ministry

The first three evangelistic outreach ministries of the Seventh-day Adventist Church were publishing, medical, and educational. Years before Seventh-day Adventists were officially organized into a church, they began to print gospel literature. In July, 1849, Ellen White encouraged her husband James White to invest what money they had to publish a small magazine, *The Present Truth.* She had seen in vision that this little paper would become as streams of light going around the world. A short time later the paper became the *Adventist Review and Sabbath Herald,* published by the Review and Herald Publishing Association. In the early 1980s the General Conference of Seventh-day Adventists became the publisher of the magazine that we know today as the *Adventist Review.* The *Adventist Review* remains one of the oldest continuously-published magazines in America. We now also have *Adventist World* which has a monthly circulation of 1.5 million copies.

In 1874 James White began to publish the *Signs of the Times* in Oakland, California. He intended it as a weekly newspaper "to be an expositor of the prophecies, a report of the signs of our times, and also a family, religious, and general newspaper for the household." The circulation of this missionary journal grew to the point that it became feasible to begin another publishing house, the Pacific Press Publishing Association. Pacific Press still publishes *Signs* to this day.

Today, hundreds of publishing operations and huge web presses around the world produce millions of pieces of Christian literature that share the message God has entrusted to Seventh-day Adventists for this critical time in earth's history.

When you read the *Adventist Review* and other literature published by the church, and when you send subscriptions of the *Signs of the Times* to non-Adventist friends and relatives, or share other Adventist literature with them, *you practice Habit Three of Highly Contagious Adventists.* Practicing this habit joins you with millions of others in the worldwide Adventist movement who are seeking to grow in Christ and to share the good news He has for this generation as we prepare for His soon return.

4. Medical Ministry

When Jesus healed people physically, it often opened their minds to His spiritual teachings. God directed Seventh-day Adventists to follow this pattern. Through visions God gave to Ellen White, and through her books on health which contained concepts far ahead of her time, the church developed a medical missionary work that has impacted the health of millions around the world and opened hearts to hear and receive the gospel.

The first Adventist health center was established in Battle Creek, Michigan, in 1866. It later became the world famous Battle Creek Sanitarium visited by U.S. Presidents and foreign dignitaries alike. Within 40 years the church had established 77 medical sanitariums and treatment facilities worldwide, many of which had nursing schools attached to them. In 1895 the church established its first medical school, American Medical Missionary College, in Battle Creek. A few years later as a result of divine guidance, great faith, and a series of miracles, the flagship medical institution of the church was established in Loma Linda, California.

In 1904 none of this seemed possible. The Loma Linda property, priced at $110,000, was too expensive. Then within the year the desperate sellers dropped the price to $40,000. They were asking for only $5,000 down, $5,000 a month for the next two months, and $5,000 in another four months, with the final $20,000 to be paid off over three years. This seemingly modest sum was an enormous stretch for the already financially strained resources of the Southern California Conference.

The Southern California Conference decided to refuse the offer. Yet God had shown this property to Ellen White in vision. So she and John Burden encouraged local lay members to contribute their own money to complete the down payment, trusting that God would provide the rest. Their faith was justified. With the creditors about to foreclose on the due date for the second payment, the postman brought a letter from Atlantic City, New Jersey, with a bank draft for $5000, the exact amount needed on the very day it was due! The donation had been solicited by Ellen White from a personal friend. With God's continued blessings, the Conference paid off the entire loan before the end of the first year, resulting in an additional discount in the price.

Originally named "The College of Medical Evangelists" in keeping with its evangelistic mission, Loma Linda University medical school is now known and respected around the world as a healing center for body and soul. Thousands of physicians, nurses, dentists, and other health professionals trained at Loma Linda have gone all over the world in service for God and humanity. A Veterans Hospital was built in Loma Linda in the 1970s primarily, it has been reported, because wherever President Richard Nixon traveled in the world, the best quality medical care available to him and his staff was operated by Seventh-day Adventists.

In addition to Loma Linda University medical school and hospital, the church operates over 600 medical institutions and several medical universities worldwide. Local Adventist communities around the world conduct thousands of health education classes (smoking cessation, nutrition and cooking, stress management, etc.) each year.

You can personally practice Habit Four of Highly Contagious Adventists in three ways:

1) by living by the health principles advocated by the Church,

2) by sharing these principles with others as God grants you opportunity, and

3) by getting involved in the health outreach ministry of your church and touching people's lives at a felt-need level, which may open the door for you to share the gospel with them.

5. Educational Ministry

In 1874, only eleven years after officially organizing as a church, Seventh-day Adventists founded Battle Creek College primarily to train pastors and teachers to staff Seventh-day Adventist churches and schools. Ellen White strongly advocated that the church establish such schools, from elementary to college level, to provide wholesome, well-rounded Christian education. She wrote two books promoting Christian education.

One story represents many miraculous divine leadings in the establishment of the educational work around the world.

In 1893 the church in Australia, with a membership of barely 1,000, set out to do the impossible—to start a higher education missionary training school. The Brettville Estate in New South Wales was economically priced, but a government soil expert called in to inspect the property remarked that the soil was so poor that a bandicoot (a marsupial like a rabbit) crossing the land would have to carry his lunch with him. Yet Ellen White had been shown in a dream that this land could be productive. As they visited the tract of land, she asked the group to join her in prayer. She laid the matter of the property before God and also prayed most earnestly for Brother McCullah who was suffering from tuberculosis. This man felt something like an electric shock pass through his body that restored him to health. This seemed to them like a sign and the property was purchased. Avondale College was begun and the land yielded bountifully, providing sustenance for students and staff.

Over the years Avondale College has sent out scores of missionaries, pastors, teachers, and other workers in God's cause. Sanitarium Health Food Company, which was established on the same site in the 1890s, today controls a leading share of the consumer cereal market in Australia and New Zealand. It has become a major source of financial support for Adventist mission work in that region of the world.

A major four-year research project was launched in 2006–2007 (www.cognitivegenesis.org) studying 30,000 students (grades 3–9, 11) in Adventist schools in all conferences in the North American Division. The data received from the first two years of that research revealed that on average Adventist students scored half a grade level higher than the national average on all grade levels for all subjects tested. The results were the same for small and large schools, small and large class sizes, and for single grade and multi-grade rooms. Your local church school may be the best school in the world for your child. It's also one of the most powerful evangelistic tools the church has.

Today the Seventh-day Adventist Church operates the largest Protestant school system in the world. In developing countries, the church often establishes medical clinics and schools even before it builds churches. Thus it lives out its commitment to follow the pattern of Jesus' ministry—minister to people's felt needs and win their confidence. Then bid them to follow Him.

You practice Habit Five of Highly Contagious Adventists when you support your local church school and the mission program of the church, when you send your children to an Adventist school or help your grandchildren or a worthy student attend. As you do your part, you become part of the worldwide movement to defeat Satan's efforts to capture young minds. By supporting Adventist education, you make it possible for young people to be trained in the School of Christ.

6. Stewardship

The extraordinary multifaceted missionary activities of the Seventh-day Adventist Church have been made possible by the extraordinary benevolence of its members. It was their sacrificial giving that enabled the small group of Sabbath-keeping Adventist Christians to become a worldwide movement within a few decades. One story illustrates this spirit, and the power of many small contributions adding up to great gains for Christ's kingdom.

In the late 1880s the General Conference, inspired by the missionary work of John Tay on Pitcairn Island, voted to purchase a missionary ship for the South Pacific islands. However, the great cost of building and equipping a mission ship was daunting.

Pitcairn was populated by descendants of the sailors who mutinied on the British ship Bounty, and it seems that God had a plan for their evangelization. The cause was taken up by the Sabbath School Association, which dedicated all the adults' and children's offerings for the first half of 1890 to this project. Coast to coast pennies and nickels flowed in for "our missionary ship." Later that year the new ship their offerings had purchased, the "Pitcairn," arrived at Pitcairn Island. Within a month all 126 inhabitants of the island were baptized in one of the rock-bound coastal pools. After organizing a Sabbath School and church, the ship and its missionary crew headed for their next destination, Tahiti.

As reports of the success of the Pitcairn reached the children in the U.S., Sabbath Schools were filled with happy laughter and singing. Together, Sabbath School offerings had accomplished what some had thought impossible.

Such stories of spontaneous giving abound in early Adventist history, but it was "Systematic Benevolence," "SB," or more affectionately, "Sister Betsy," that was the recommended plan from very early in our church's history. It eventually came to include 10% of income for tithe, and an additional dedicated percentage of income for other offerings (world missions, Sabbath School, etc.). It was the Adventist response to Jesus' instruction not to lay up treasures on earth, but in heaven.

Tithe submitted to a local church supports full-time gospel workers, both in that local conference and around the world. Adventist pastors are supported by the tithe, and their salaries are not based on the size of their church. Pastors in both large and small congregations are equally reimbursed, based on the cost of living in the areas they serve. Offerings given over and above the tithe support the local church and other designated ministries. When you systematically give your tithe and offerings to God, you are supporting the growth of God's kingdom locally and around the world. You are investing your treasure in heaven. You are practicing *Habit Six of Highly Contagious Adventists.*

7. Community Service

Ellen White's personal example, and her books *Christian Service* and *Welfare Ministry*, have contributed to the social conscience of the church and have served as a motivating force in its expansive humanitarian commitment to those who are impoverished and suffering in the world.

Beginning in 1874 the church's ministry to the poor and suffering was referred to at the local church level as the Dorcas Society (named after a New Testament woman who ministered to the poor—Acts 9:36–39). It was later renamed Adventist Community Services.

In 1919 a worldwide offering was taken to assist Adventists in the war-devastated countries of Europe. Mobilizations to assist areas of the world stricken by natural disasters increased over the years. In 1944–1945 disaster relief efforts assisted 41 countries and island groups that had been devastated by World War II in Europe, Asia, and Africa.

In 1956 the General Conference established the Seventh-day Adventist Welfare Service (SAWS), which in 1984 was renamed the Adventist Development and Relief Agency (ADRA). As the global humanitarian arm of the Seventh-day Adventist Church, ADRA's stated mission is "to follow Christ's example by being a voice for, serving, and partnering with those in need."

ADRA provides both long-term development assistance to address social injustice and deprivation in developing countries, and emergency management initiatives to provide aid to disaster survivors. In addition, it engages in many activities to improve the quality of life of those in need. For example: building health clinics in Africa, assisting hurricane victims in Central America, teaching hygiene and health to children in Asia, and promoting awareness of worldwide humanitarian needs through ADRA's Global Village in the United States.

ADRA operates today in 125 countries. It annually serves approximately 23 million people with over $60 million in development, relief services, and aid (in 2011). ADRA is currently one of the leading non-governmental relief organizations in the world. In 1997 the agency was granted General Consultative Status by the United Nations, a unique opportunity giving ADRA added voice in the international community.

When you contribute to ADRA, when you support the local community services ministry of your church either by monetary contributions or by volunteering your services to help others, when you give to relieve suffering or lend a hand to help a neighbor in need in the spirit of Jesus, you are *practicing Habit Seven of Highly Contagious Adventists.*

ACTIVITY (1)

How many of the Seven Habits of Highly Contagious Adventists can you remember?

B. Testimonies

1. Charlie

I became a Seventh-day Adventist in Ely, Nevada when I was 23 years old. I took Bible studies from an Adventist and became convinced that Adventists were teaching the truths of the Bible. On Sabbaths we met in a house church. Sometimes there were only two or three of us there. On a special Sabbath, we may have 8–10 attend. Even though I had been told that there were millions of Seventh-day Adventists in the world, that didn't seem very real to me. At times I would get discouraged attending our little group. When I attended a camp meeting in Springville, Utah with several hundred other Seventh-day Adventists, I experienced for the first time that the church was more than our little house church in Ely. Then I got to attend a General Conference session in San Francisco. Seeing 50,000 Adventists from all over the world meeting together in one place, and hearing the mission reports from all over the world, was one of the greatest experiences of my life. I went back to my little house church with a whole new vision of the world movement I was truly part of. It gave me much more confidence in talking to others about what I believe.

2. Helen

The church I grew up in was very small. I attended public school, so I didn't have the advantage of a Christian education. I often felt like my little church was an embarrassment to me, and I used to hope that my friends wouldn't find out that I was a Seventh-day Adventist. I'll never forget the day that someone from South America came to our church and told about what was happening in the church there. He told the most amazing stories of how churches were growing by thousands as a result of what the Holy Spirit was doing through Bible studies the members were giving and through miracles in answer to prayer. Something happened to me that day. I now felt "proud" to be a Seventh-day Adventist, and wanted my friends to know what God was doing through my church. Even though the same things weren't happening in my local church that I heard the man from South America tell us was happening in his area, I still felt like I was part of something big that God was doing in the world. And I began to believe that He just might be able to do something big in my community also in answer to prayer and my own involvement.

3. Briana

I've been active in my church for as long as I can remember. But in all honesty I often wondered if my efforts were making any difference. It seemed like our church didn't change much over the years. Still many of the same people and about the same size, no matter what we did. But I kept reading in the Adventist Review about what God was doing in other places. And one day I realized that by being faithful with my contributions and ministry in my local church, I was actually part of the great things that were happening all over the world. Somehow that transformed my attitude toward my own local ministry. It gave me a joy and enthusiasm for my ministry I hadn't had before. I feel so honored to have my little part in what God is doing all over the world.

4. Christopher

For over ten years I have been a member of a large Adventist church, over a thousand members. We're a very active church. We sponsor many ministries to our community and have evangelistic meetings nearly every year. We generally have a positive image in our community. Many people in our community have benefited from our felt need health education classes and community service programs. I feel a humble pride in letting people know I'm a member of our church. Because of all this, it would be easy for me to focus all my attention and resources on my local church. But our Sabbath School program includes a monthly report from the mission field via a Mission Spotlight video. These reports remind me that the Adventist movement is much bigger than my local church, and that I have the responsibility and privilege of supporting by my prayers and mission offerings what God is doing through His church around the world.

C. Your Contagious Adventist Mission Statement

Sample from Skip:

I have heard God's call and have put my faith in Jesus Christ as my Savior and Lord, and as the sole basis of my eternal salvation. My life goal now is to use the gifts, time, and passions God gives me by His grace to exert the most positive influence I can on my family and others God gives me influence with. I want my life to encourage them to accept Jesus as Savior and Lord of their lives and to become influences themselves who will in turn encourage still others to do the same in an ever widening circle until Jesus comes.

The principles of the Contagious Adventist course—knowing the unique truths God has entrusted to our Church for this hour in history, recognizing and creating creative openings to share those truths, sharing the testimony of the difference God and His truths have made in my life, and inviting people to make decisions that are appropriate to the occasion—are tools I want to use to help me achieve my goal of influencing others in every way I can for God's kingdom. Under the influence of the Holy Spirit and through prayer, the seven Habits of Highly Contagious Adventists are spheres of activity I have the privilege to be engaged in to help me be the contagious influence for His kingdom that I want to be.

Sample from Marilyn:

Born and raised in an Adventist home, the gift of salvation through Jesus and the certainty of His Second Coming have been the constant focus of my life. My life mission is to be a link in the chain of influence that draws others to Jesus Christ and the distinctive truths of the Seventh-day Adventist Church. God has given me the tools of friendship, prayer, hospitality, letter-writing, and a ready smile. I have committed these gifts to a Contagious Adventist ministry of sharing my faith in my immediate neighborhood and with those who are brought into my life by divine appointment.

Sample from Dick:

I am a Contagious Adventist because I want to share my Jesus with everyone. I want them to come to know Jesus in all His love and grace and faithfulness. I want them to recognize Him in their lives, molding and shaping them, transforming them into the wonderful miracle He created them to be. None of this happens by chance. It is a choice we each must make, but it is a choice encouraged and guided by the Holy Spirit, drawing us ever deeper and deeper into a loving relationship with Jesus. Bible study is an essential part of this process. We grow closer to Jesus by studying His Word, finding in Bible stories a fuller, richer portrait of our Savior. Sharing our testimonies of how our friendship with Jesus has shaped and blessed our lives is another part. Sharing our testimonies reassures us that Jesus through the Holy Spirit is still actively involved in our lives. What He has done for others He is ever seeking to do for us. So I am a Contagious Adventist because I want to share my understanding of Jesus as revealed in the Bible and through my life's journey so that others may more fully come to know the breadth and length, the height and depth of the love of God through Jesus my Lord.

Sample from Esther:

My mission statement can be summed up in the words of an early Advent hymn.

> *I am bound for the Promised Land, I am bound for the Promised Land;*
> *O who will come and go with me? I am bound for the Promised Land.*

Because of God's grace I know where I am going and I want to take others with me. For that reason I throw myself into the work of the Master knowing that nothing I do for Him is a waste of time or effort. I am intentional about how I live my life—making myself available every moment of the day to be used by the Holy Spirit. I want to recognize and create contagious Adventist moments. My conversations will be focused on Cultivating the soil, Planting the seed, and Reaping the harvest—CPR for eternal life. I believe that the message of the Seventh-day Adventist movement, however yet incomplete, is the highest, fullest, and best expression of the lovely character of God that the world has ever known. I want others to join the movement so more people have the chance to respond. I will not wait for opportunities to come to me: I will seek them out. My dad (whom I long to see in the resurrection) taught me that a woman's place is in her Father's business—so I am taking the place God has designed for me, for such a time as this.

ACTIVITY (2) (3) (4)

We invite you to reflect on what you have learned and experienced over these nine sessions....

Write your own Contagious Adventist mission statement.

D. HOMEWORK: The adventure continues...

"The disciples were to begin their work where they were [Jerusalem]. The hardest and most unpromising field was not to be passed by. So every one of Christ's workers is to begin where he is. In our own families [and our own local church] may be souls hungry for sympathy, starving for the bread of life. There may be children to be trained for Christ. There are heathen at our very doors. Let us do faithfully the work that is nearest. Then let our efforts be extended as far as God's hand may lead the way. The work of many may appear to be restricted by circumstances; but, wherever it is, if performed with faith and diligence it will be felt to the uttermost parts of the earth. Christ's work when upon earth appeared to be confined to a narrow field, but multitudes from all lands heard His message. God often uses the simplest means to accomplish the greatest results. It is His plan that every part of His work shall depend on every other part, as a wheel within a wheel, all acting in harmony. The humblest worker, moved by the Holy Spirit, will touch invisible chords, whose vibrations will ring to the ends of the earth, and make melody through eternal ages....

"[Christ] made full provision for the prosecution of the work, and took upon Himself the responsibility for its success. So long as they [His disciples and us] obeyed His word, and worked in connection with Him, they could not fail....He bade them, Labor in confidence, for the time will never come when I will forsake you." *Desire of Ages*, pp. 822–823

APPENDIX A

QUESTIONS/RESPONSES
Session 1—None

Session 2—Jesus Is Lord

1. Q. I tried to have a relationship with God once, but it didn't work for me.

Suggested Response:

a. What does "having a relationship with God" mean to you? What were you looking for that didn't work?

b. "What did you believe about God? What kind of being did you understand Him to be?"

c. I've had ups and downs in my experience with God also, but the Bible says that God doesn't give up on us. That's good news for me. Would you be interested in talking more about this?

d. I've felt that way before myself. But the Bible says in John 6:37 that Jesus will turn no one away who comes to Him. It's promises like that that keep me going. Maybe we could talk more about this?

e. Would you be interested in having a relationship with God if it were assured that it could work?

2. Q. I was active in my church some time back, but I've kind of gotten away from it. I really need to get back.

Suggested Response:

a. How can I help you? I'd love to have that opportunity.

b. What was it like when you were involved before?

c. Some people think that before they could come back to God and their church they would have to make major changes in their lives. But that's not the case. The way back to God is simply to come, just as you are. God can take it from there.

d. Well, let me be the first to give you that opportunity. I'd love for you to visit my church sometime. What are the chances that you might be able to come this week, as my special guest?

3. Q. How do you actually have a relationship with God?

Suggested Response:

That's a very good question, maybe the most important question in life. The Bible says that anyone who comes to God "must believe that He is, and that He is a rewarder of those who diligently seek Him" (Hebrews 11:6 NKJV). I know that you believe in God. He also wants you to know that if you want a relationship with Him, and will take steps to have a relationship with Him and put your trust in Him, He will personally guarantee that nothing will be able to stop that from happening, except your own choice to stop seeking Him again (John 10:27–29; Rom 8:35–39). (At that point you could share the Bridge illustration and, if appropriate, invite them to accept Jesus.)

How do you have a relationship with anyone? (Discuss that for a bit and then make the application.) A relationship with God is developed by studying about Him in the Bible, spending time talking with Him in prayer, learning about Him from others who know Him, and spending time with people who gather to worship and learn more of Him.

4. Q. I have a weakness that keeps me from staying with God. I just don't know how to overcome it.

Suggested Response:

There's not an honest believer on this planet who will not tell you that they struggle with weaknesses. Even the Apostle Paul said that sin dwelling in him kept him from doing things he knew he should and made him do the things he shouldn't (Romans 7:15–24). But while he testified that he was not perfect, he also said that he continued to strive to do God's will and to trust His salvation to God

(Philippians 3:12–14). That is what the gospel is all about. It's God promising to do for us what we cannot do for ourselves. Jesus said that if we will keep coming to Him, He will assure us of a place of rest with Him in His eternal kingdom (Matthew 11:28). God has assured us, "My grace is sufficient for you, for my power is made perfect in weakness" (2 Corinthians 12:9).

Session 3—The Great Controversy

1. Q. Have you ever wondered how there could be so much suffering in the world if a good God exists?

Suggested Response:

The opening chapters of the book of Job reveal that Satan is the cause of the suffering in the world. Satan questions humanity's obedience to God and challenges God before the other inhabited worlds to prove that people will uphold God's righteousness despite immense suffering. God chooses Job to uphold His honor. Satan proceeds to inflict every conceivable calamity upon Job, except Job's own death. Job remains faithful to God and for this is eventually doubly blessed.

This conflict is played out in each of our lives with Satan inflicting countless sufferings upon us in an effort to make us turn away from God. God permits our suffering as He did with Job so we can learn the true nature of evil and freely choose to forsake it and follow God.

God does not leave us alone in this struggle. If we put our trust in Jesus, He who has defeated Satan by His life, death, and resurrection will deliver us from all evil. Eventually Satan and all evil will be destroyed and there will be no more suffering or death (Revelation 20:14).

2. Q. Do you think that hurricanes, tornados, and other "natural" disasters are really "acts of God"?

Suggested Response:

The Bible says that sin and suffering are the work of Satan, not God (e.g., Job 1–2). It also says that death, the catastrophic consequence of "natural" disasters, is the result of sin (Romans 5:12). It describes nature itself as suffering from the consequence of humanity's sin and awaiting the world's redemption at the Second Coming of Jesus (Romans 8:19–23). So, since "natural" disasters and the suffering they inflict are the result of sin, they surely are not "acts of God."

Yet how can a good God allow such disasters to afflict the innocent as well as the guilty? We do not know the full answer, but we do have God's assurance that if we trust Him, He will work through all experiences of life, even the tragic ones, to accomplish a good end (John 9:1–3; Romans 8:28). And we await in hope for the promised redemption at the Second Coming of Jesus Christ in which all things will be made new and suffering will be no more.

3. Q. Have you ever wondered whether there is some meaning to our lives?

Suggested Response:

If you believe that we are alive by accident or chance, then it is hard to believe life has any meaning other than mere existence. We live, procreate, and die and the next generation takes over. But if we exist due to the loving plan of a Creator who wanted us, as the Bible describes, then life has great meaning. The Bible says that God made us in His image, for His glory, and with plans for our present and eternal happiness (Genesis 1:26–27; Isaiah 43:7; Jeremiah 29:12).

That means our life's purpose is to develop a relationship with God through which He can work out His eternal plan for us. God initiates this relationship. He comes to us—through His testimony in the Bible, through providential events, and through people who love and care for us—and draws us into a loving relationship with Him (Isaiah 45:22; Matthew 11:28; Revelation 3:20). When we respond to God by putting our trust in Him and His Son Jesus and making a commitment to obey Him, He makes us His ambassador to our world, commissioned with His authority to proclaim His name before all peoples and to call them into this same loving relationship

(2 Corinthians 2:14; 5:20). Thus our life becomes filled with meaning and bears fruit in eternal life (John 3:16; 14:21, 23; 1 John 5:12).

4. Q. But I still don't see why God didn't kill Satan, or even Adam and Eve, as soon as they sinned, and then start over. Think of all the suffering it would have saved.

Suggested Response:

The answer seems to lie in the character of God who values the freedom, trust, confidence, loyalty, and love of His creation. If a U.S. President were falsely accused of embezzling millions of dollars and the President had his accuser executed on the spot, would that engender the confidence of the U.S. population in general? Likely not. Rage maybe. Possibly even fear. But hardly confidence and trust.

Though Satan had become a cosmic terrorist, God allowed him the freedom to demonstrate on this earth what his alternative plan for running the universe would ultimately lead to. The adage is true: Give a cat enough rope, and it will hang itself.

Had God destroyed sin prematurely, His loyal universe might not have understood the hideous consequences of its reign. Love and trust are best preserved and guaranteed through demonstration rather than force. By comparing God's love with Satan's tyranny, people will come to understand that God's unrestricted love offers the best promise for a safe and secure universe.

5. Q. Still, it seems so unfair that because Adam sinned, we have to suffer so much. I wasn't responsible and yet I was put into the middle of this mess without any choice.

Suggested Response:

That's true, but the Bible says God takes all of that into account. It says that as we have compassion on our own children, so God has compassion on us, "for he knows how we are formed; he remembers that we are dust" (Psalm 103:14–15). And as unfair as it was that we were born into this world of sin, it was even more unfair that

Jesus had to come here and suffer with us and die for us. At least we have sinned and deserve some of what we get, but Jesus was totally innocent. He came because if He had been in our place He would have wanted someone to do that for Him. That's what God's love is all about.

The Bible says, "Where sin abounded, grace abounded much more" (Romans 5:20). That means that as much damage as sin has done to us, God intervenes to an even greater degree to heal the wounds sin has inflicted and to restore us to the hope of eternal life in Paradise with Him as we put our trust in Him and follow Him.

6. Q. Can't I just be a good person without becoming a Christian?

Suggested Response:

Jesus said that without Him we can do nothing of worth in God's sight (John 15:4–5). More than that, without Jesus we cannot withstand the power of Satan. The Bible says that we have been so thoroughly affected by sin, that even the "good" we do apart from God is as filthy rags in His sight (Isaiah 64:6).

Becoming a Christian is making a decision to stay united to the One who alone can save you and to become actively involved with His family, the church, that He Himself established to be your support group and through which you could serve others in ways that will assist them in becoming or remaining followers of God themselves.

7. Q. Why can't I just serve God on my own without having to join a church?

Suggested Response:

Joining a church is a matter of obedience to God. Jesus said that He established the church (Matthew 16:18). It's not a man-made institution. Jesus said that unless we are born of water (baptized) and the Spirit (converted in heart by the Holy Spirit), we will not enter His kingdom (John 3:5). Paul said that when we are baptized, we become members of Christ's body, the church (1 Corinthians 12:13; Colossians 1:18).

The church certainly is not perfect, because it is made up of imperfect people like us, but it is God's instrument to take His message to the world. Through the church we can combine our personal and financial resources to do much more good in the world than if we were isolated. And isolated we would each one be more vulnerable to the assaults of Satan, just like a hot coal if removed from the bed of coals in the fireplace will quickly go out.

8. Q. Why did God create us with free choice? Why didn't He just make us so we would follow Him and do His will?

Suggested Response:

The Bible says that God made Adam and Eve in His image, which means in part that their natural inclination was to love and follow God (Genesis 1:26–27). But He also gave them free will, because we cannot really experience love unless we are free to choose.

The Bible says that Adam and Eve freely chose to disobey God, and as a result all their children, including us, were born with sinful natures that do not naturally seek God (Romans 3:10–11; 5:12). That sounds very unfair, that we are born with sinful natures, and it is unfair, but God more than evened the score. Jesus Christ came and lived the perfect life that we *should have* lived but *could not* (because we were born in sin). Then He attributed His own perfect life, His own righteousness, to us as a free gift (2 Corinthians 5:21). Jesus' death is also attributed to us in place of the eternal death we should die, so that through His death we have the forgiveness of our sins. The free gift God has given us in Jesus' life and death for us has offered us "much more" than everything we had lost through our birth into sin (Romans 5:10–20).

Only when we realize love is a matter of choice can we understand the depths of the Father's love that He would choose to give His only Son so that not one of us need be lost. It is this knowledge that should bind us so strongly to our God—our freedom of choice was purchased at so great a price by His Son.

Session 4—The Sabbath

1. Q. The Sabbath was given so long ago. How can we know which day is really the seventh-day Sabbath of the Bible?

Suggested Response:

a. Good Friday and Easter celebrations have come down to us from early Christian history. The Bible identifies the seventh-day Sabbath as Saturday—the day between Good Friday, when Jesus died, and Easter Sunday, when Jesus rose from the dead (Luke 23:52; 24:2). So history itself, as well as the Bible, establishes that the seventh-day Sabbath is Saturday.

b. The Jews, who have worshiped on the seventh-day Sabbath ever since the command was given in the Ten Commandments, still worship on Saturday today.

c. In 105 languages of the world, the name for the seventh day of the week, which we call Saturday, is "Sabbath."

d. There is an astronomical basis for each of the major time divisions: year (journey of the earth around the sun); month (one complete full moon cycle); day (one complete rotation of the earth on its axis). But there is no corresponding astronomical basis for the seven-day week which has been passed down through human history and is the worldwide standard still today. Attempts by various nations to change the seven-day weekly cycle have all failed. Where did the seven-day week originate? The most reasonable explanation is that it came from the Bible's story of creation of which the Sabbath was specifically given by God to be a reminder (Genesis 2:1–3; Exodus 31:17; Ezekiel 20:20).

2. Q. Wasn't the Sabbath given just for the Jews?

Suggested Response:

a. The Sabbath was created by Jesus during the creation week, long before the Jewish nation came into existence (Genesis 2:1–3).

b. Throughout the Old Testament the Sabbath was God's gift to bless Gentiles as well as Jews. "And *foreigners* who bind themselves to the Lord, to serve him, to love the name of the Lord, and to worship him, all who keep the Sabbath without desecrating it, and who hold fast to my covenant—these I will bring to my holy mountain and give them joy in my house of prayer...for my house will be called a house of prayer for *all nations*" (Isaiah 56:6–7).

c. Jesus Himself said that "the Sabbath was made for man," not simply for the Jews (Mark 2:28).

3. Q. But doesn't the Bible say somewhere that we are supposed to worship God on "the Lord's Day"?

Suggested Response:

God called the seventh-day Sabbath "My holy day" (Isaiah 58:13). Jesus called Himself the "Lord of the Sabbath" (Matthew 12:8). So in the Bible, the Lord's Day is the seventh-day Sabbath.

4. Q. Doesn't Romans 14:5–6 say that the important thing is that you are convinced in your own mind about what day you should worship on, not the actual day itself, and that if you believe there's no special day at all for worship, then that's the truth for you?

Suggested Response:

a. Paul does not have in mind here the seventh-day Sabbath which God instituted at creation and reiterated many times through-out Scripture, and which Paul himself observed throughout his lifetime.

In Romans 14:1 Paul says he is discussing "disputable matters." The seventh-day Sabbath God gave in the Ten Commandments was never a "disputable matter." The "special days" Paul was referring to in Romans 14:5–6 were the ceremonial feast days and ceremonial holy days, such as the Passover. The question was, "Is it wrong for a Christian, perhaps one with a Jewish background, to still observe the Passover, for instance?" Paul's answer was, In such "disputable matters," let each decide for themselves.

Evangelical scholar Matthew Henry writes in his commentary on these verses: "Those who thought themselves still under some kind of obligation by the ceremonial law, esteemed *one day above another*, kept up a respect to the times of the passover, pentecost, new moons, and feasts of tabernacles; thought those days better than other days, and solemnized them accordingly with, particular observances, binding themselves to some religious rest and exercise on those days. Those who knew that all these things were abolished and done away by Christ's coming, esteemed *every day* alike. We must understand it with an exception of the Lord's day, which all Christians unanimously observed; but they make no account, took no notice, of those antiquated festivals of the Jews." Matthew Henry, *Matthew Henry's Commentary on the Whole Bible* (Wilmington, Delaware: Sovereign Grace Publishers, 1972), 2:995–996.

There is no sin in observing such ceremonies as long as one realizes that Christ, to whom they pointed, has now come. On the other hand, Jewish Christians should not feel that Gentile Christians have to attend such feasts. Let each be convinced in one's own mind about such things.

Even today there are Jewish Christians who observe the Jewish holidays, albeit with a Christian interpretation to them. This is the very kind of thing Paul is referring to in Romans 14:5.

b. Most churches that try to use this text to prove that it does not matter if someone keeps the seventh-day Sabbath or not do not apply it consistently themselves. If a member of a Sunday-keeping church takes a job that requires Sunday work, and so shifts their day of worship to Tuesday, it is not likely that their pastor will say, "That's fine, just so you are fully convinced in your mind about it." Most likely the parishioner will be told that it is important for them and their family to worship with their congregation on Sunday, even if they have to change jobs to do so.

5. Q. But I thought Colossians 2:13–15 says that the Ten Commandments were nailed to the cross when Jesus died and do not apply to us anymore.

Suggested Response:

What it actually says is, "He [Christ] forgave us all our sins, having canceled the written code, with its regulations, that was against us and that stood opposed to us; he took it away, nailing it to the cross."

The original Greek word for "written code" ("handwriting" NKJV) signified a "certificate of indebtedness" made out in the debtor's own handwriting. One might say, "I'll give you this loan, but I'll need your 'handwriting' (signature) for it." Verses 13–15 identify this indebtedness as being our sins which are in every way against us, and which Jesus took away when He died on the cross for us.

The "regulations" or "ordinances" of the written code which "was against us, which was contrary to us," can be understood in two ways. First it refers to the weaknesses of the ceremonial system as Hebrews 7–10 enumerates them (cannot take away sins, cannot make the conscience perfect, an annual reminder of sins, etc.). Secondly, it signifies the human misappropriation of God's moral law into a system of works righteousness (as Galatians 3–5 enumerates). Rightly understood and applied to one's life, Christ's death for our sins brings an end to both of these systems as inadequate to accomplish the forgiveness of our sins.

6. Q. Doesn't Colossians 2:16 say that we should not let anyone judge us as to whether we worship on a Sabbath or not?

Suggested Response:

The Sabbaths referred to in Colossians 2:16 are qualified in verse 17 as those that "are a shadow of the things that were to come; the reality, however, is found in Christ."

There were two kinds of Sabbaths in the Bible. The first kind was the seventh-day weekly Sabbath instituted by God in Eden before sin entered the picture. This was the Sabbath reiterated in the Ten Commandments and which God referred to as "my holy day" (Genesis 2:1–3; Exodus 20:8–11; Isaiah 58:13–14; Mark 2:27–28; etc.). This Sabbath was observed throughout biblical history, and will be observed in the new earth. It was not "a shadow of things to come," but rather represented the timeless truth that God is our Creator and Redeemer, the One who made us and makes us holy (Exodus 31:12, 17; Ezekiel 20:12, 20).

The other kind of sabbath was the ceremonial sabbaths connected to the annual feasts that were associated with the Old Testament sanctuary ceremonial system (e.g., Leviticus 23:7–8, 21, 24, 32, 35–36). These annual, ceremonial sabbaths occurred on fixed dates of the months in which the feasts were held and so fell on different days of the week each year. (For example, our Thanksgiving is always on a Thursday, but Christmas and New Year's Day celebrations are on a fixed date on the calendar. They were mere symbolic shadows that pointed forward to the Messiah to come. The sabbaths referred to in Colossians 2:16 are these annual, ceremonial sabbaths, not the weekly Sabbath contained in the Ten Commandments.

The commentary note of the New International Study Bible on this text says: "The ceremonial laws of the OT are here referred to as the shadows (cf. Heb. 8:5; 10:1) because they symbolically depicted the coming of Christ; so any insistence on the observance of such ceremonies is a failure to recognize that their fulfillment has already taken place."

Albert Barnes, respected American Presbyterian scholar, writes in his commentary on this text: "...he [Paul] had his eye on the great number of days which were observed by the Hebrews as festivals, as part of their ceremonial and typical law, and not to the *moral* law, or the Ten Commandments. No part of the moral law—not one of the Ten Commandments could be spoken of as 'a shadow of good things to come.' These commandments are, from the nature of moral law, of perpetual and universal obligation."

7. Q. With all the calendar changes that have been made through the centuries, how can anyone know which day is the real seventh day the Bible speaks about?

Suggested Response:

There have actually been only two changes in the calendar since the days of Jesus and the apostles. In both cases the change constituted a transfer from the Julian calendar (named after Julius Caesar) to the Gregorian calendar (named after Pope Gregory).

Over the centuries the Julian calendar got increasingly out of sync with a true astronomical year, and necessitated a change to a calendar that incorporated a leap-year system to keep the calendar more accurate. In numerous European countries this took place in 1582. In English-speaking countries it occurred in 1752.

In both cases the seven-day week, as well as the sequence in the days of the week, were unaltered. In 1582 people went to bed on Thursday, October 4, and woke up on Friday, October 15. Those who made the change in 1752 went to bed on Wednesday, September 2, and woke on Thursday, September 14.

Thus we can be historically certain that the seventh-day Sabbath that Jesus and the apostles kept was the same as the seventh day of the week, Saturday, on our calendars today. In over 100 languages of the world the name of the seventh day of the week is not Saturday (named after the god Saturn by the Romans), but "Sabbath" (the name given the seventh day in the Bible).

8. Q. Isn't the teaching that the Sabbath can be kept holy only on the seventh day pure legalism?

Suggested Response:

Many initially come to respect and honor the seventh-day Sabbath out of a sheer sense of duty. They want to keep the seventh day holy simply because God commanded it. However, most who observe it by communing with God and fellowshipping with other believers eventually come to appreciate it as the precious gift and immense blessing that it is.

Legalism does not consist of the *day* on which one observes the Sabbath, but the *way* in which one observes it. Worship on Sunday could be just as legalistic as worship on Saturday, depending on the attitude and spirit of the worshipper.

9. Q. Doesn't it say in the Bible somewhere that God changed the Sabbath from the seventh day to the first day of the week?

Suggested Response:

a. Many people have tried to find such a text, but one has never been found.

b. There are only eight texts in the New Testament that even mention the first day of the week. Six of them occur in the story of the resurrection of Jesus and mention that it was early in the morning on the first day of the week that He rose (Matthew 28:1–6; Mark 16:1–6, 9; Luke 24:1–6; John 20:1–10). One says they broke bread together that day, a custom they practiced *daily* (Acts 2:46; 20:7). One says they were to set some money aside on that day for a collection that would be taken later to help the poor in Jerusalem (1 Corinthians 16:1–2). There is not one word in any of these texts about transferring the Sabbath from the seventh day to the first.

c. Many Catholic scholars have been honest enough to admit that church leaders later made the change without the authority of the Bible. Cardinal Gibbons wrote: "You may read the Bible from Genesis to Revelation, and you will not find a single line authorizing the sanctification of Sunday. The Scriptures enforce the religious observance of Saturday, a day which we never sanctify" (*The Faith of Our Fathers*, p. 89).

d. Some Catholic scholars have taunted Protestants for claiming to follow the Bible even though they observe Sunday as their day of worship, a day authorized by the Catholic Church, not the Bible. Note this challenge put forth by John A. O'Brien, professor at Notre Dame at the time: "Since Saturday, not Sunday, is specified in the Bible, isn't it curious that non-Catholics who profess to take their religion directly from the Bible and not from the Church, observe Sunday instead of Saturday? Yes, of course, it is inconsistent; but this change was made about fifteen centuries before Protestantism was born, and by that time the custom was universally observed. They have continued the custom, even though it rests upon the authority of the Catholic church and not upon an explicit text in the Bible. That observance remains as a reminder of the Mother church from which the non-Catholic sects broke away—like a boy running away from home but still carrying in his pocket a picture of his mother or a lock of her hair" ("The Faith of Millions: The Credentials of the Catholic Religion." *Our Sunday Visitor*, 1955 ed., p. 473).

10. Q. Isn't it true that rather than simply worshiping God on only one day each week, we should worship Him every day?

Suggested Response:

If you mean that we should be faithful to God every day of the week, you are absolutely right. But to worship God, in the sense in which the fourth commandment tells us to observe the Sabbath, would be impractical and even disobedient to the commandment itself. In the fourth commandment God instructs us that we are to accomplish our work activities on the first six days of the week and then on the seventh to cease from our work and observe the Sabbath, just as God Himself did during the creation week (Exodus 20:8–11).

11. Q. What in the world do you do all day Saturday?

Suggested Responses:

a. I have to admit that when I first began to observe the Sabbath, it wasn't easy because I was so used to working in some way practically every day of my life—if not at the job, then on the house, the yard, the car, etc. But after a while I really began to see the beauty of the Sabbath. Now I look forward to it. I join my church family in the worship of God. Then I have extra time for my family and friends. Our conversations are often on a higher spiritual plane than they are during the week. I think the sacredness of the day encourages that.

b. I've grown up with the Sabbath. I have good memories as a child going to Sabbath School in the morning. That's equivalent to Sunday School with lots of stories, singing, Bible study, etc. They made it really fun for us kids. Then we usually had a special Sabbath lunch with a special treat of some kind. In the afternoon we often did something special as a family that it seems we didn't have time to do during the week. Sometimes we would visit someone who was sick, or get involved in some other activity of the church. Now that I have a family of my own, I try to make Sabbath a special day for them too.

c. I can really understand your question. When I was growing up my parents didn't let me do much on the Sabbath. It wasn't the day I looked forward to the most. I enjoyed the activities at the church. But the rest of the day I wasn't allowed to play my normal children's games and I don't think my parents understood how hard that was for a kid. But I used to visit a friend some Sabbaths whose parents knew how to make Sabbath really special. They would take us on walks in the woods or by a lake or in a nice park. Sometimes we would watch a nature video or play special games that directed our minds to God and the Bible. I've never forgotten that and have tried to make Sabbath special in such ways for my own children.

12. **Q.** How could so many Christian leaders and churches be wrong? If the Sabbath truly is on Saturday, wouldn't people like Billy Graham and Max Lucado be worshiping on that day?

Suggested Response:

That's a really good question, and one that I have wondered about many times myself. And I can't answer for Billy Graham. And the Bible tells me that I won't be judged by what Billy Graham teaches, but by what the Bible teaches. I trust God to work in Billy's life in His own time and way.

Once in Jesus' day the Pharisees sent a posse of temple guards to spy on Jesus, arrest Him, and bring Him back for trial. When the guards found Him, they were so impressed by His message to the crowds that they left Him alone and returned empty-handed. When they were interrogated, they told their superiors that they had never heard a man speak such profound words. Seeking to discredit Jesus, the Pharisees shouted back, "'Has any of the rulers or of the Pharisees believed in him?'" (John 7:47). In other words, if the prominent religious leaders do not believe in Him, He must be an imposter!

Jesus said, "'My sheep listen to my voice; I know them, and they follow me'" (John 10:27). There are many good people in the world who teach many good things and help many people. But there is only one voice that is ultimately safe to listen to, and only one Person safe to follow completely. I want to be a follower of Jesus and I believe you do too.

13. Q. As a practical matter, what difference does it make what day we worship on?

Suggested Response:

That's an excellent question. And for us it's simply a matter of obedience to God. The book of Revelation says that God's last-day people will be those who "obey God's commandments and remain faithful to Jesus" (Revelation 14:12).

If your son or daughter were contemplating moving in with a friend of the opposite sex, and you could not convince them purely on logical grounds why it is better to wait until marriage, wouldn't you want them to simply trust God enough to obey His word even though they could not see the logic of it at the time? It is somewhat that way with the Sabbath. There is a logic that is gained through experience that may not convince someone who has not experienced it yet. But bottom line, Jesus says, "'If you love me, you will obey what I command'" (John 14:15). Some things are more a matter of love and obedience than they are a matter of logic.

14. Q. But shouldn't we worship on the first day of the week as a memorial of Jesus' resurrection?

Suggested Response:

Excellent question. Jesus' resurrection makes all the difference in the world. Without His resurrection, His death would have meant very little.

But Jesus gave us a symbol of His resurrection when He gave us baptism. The Bible says, "We were therefore buried with him through baptism into death in order that, just as Christ was raised from the dead through the glory of the Father, we too may live a new life" (Romans 6:4).

Every communion acts as a renewal of our baptism into Jesus' death and resurrection. The Bible says, "For whenever you eat this bread and drink this cup, you proclaim the Lord's death until He comes" (1 Corinthians 11:26). Every communion not only reminds us of, and reaffirms our faith in, Jesus' sacrifice for us, but does the same in regard to His return as our resurrected Lord.

Cain's offense was offering to God a sacrifice God did not ask for. Cain may have developed beautiful symbolism around the fruit that He offered to God. But God wanted an animal sacrifice to represent the substitutionary sacrifice of the Messiah. God accepted Abel's sacrifice offered in faith, and rejected Cain's. We do not doubt that beautiful symbolism can be ascribed to the observance of the first day of the week. But that is not what God asked for. That is the bottom line for us.

Session 5—Death and Beyond

1. Q. In 2 Corinthians 5:8 Paul says, "We are confident, I say, and would prefer to be away from the body and at home with the Lord." This sure sounds like Paul anticipated that at the moment of his death he would leave his earthly body and be at home with God in heaven.

Suggested Response:

It's true that one can *interpret* the text that way, but that's not what this text actually says. In verses 1–4 of that chapter, it's quite clear that Paul is talking about exchanging his earthly body, with all of its undesirable frailties, for a heavenly one. But that entire passage (verses 1–10) does not even hint at *when* such an exchange will take place. To discover *when* that will happen, we have to look elsewhere in the Bible.

First Corinthians 15:50–54 identifies the *when*. It says that *on the day of resurrection* which will take place *at the Second Coming of Jesus*, this earthly body that is subject to corruption, illness, decay, etc., will be exchanged for an immortal, incorruptible body. At the resurrection God does not bring saved people down from heaven, but wakes them out of their sleep to give them their final reward, including a new heavenly body that is immortal and incorruptible (Revelation 22:12).

2. Q. In Philippians 1:21–24 Paul expresses his desire to depart and be with the Lord. This sounds like he looked forward to dying and going immediately to be with God.

Suggested Response:

Paul's statement in Philippians 1:21–24 merely expresses his *desire* to be relieved of the many severe trials he endured in this life (2 Corinthians 11:24–28) and to be with God. But it says nothing about whether he believed he would be with God immediately upon his death or later when God woke him at the resurrection. What Paul believed about the *timing* of when he would be in the literal presence of God is found in 1 Corinthians 15:50–54. The *timing* will occur *on the day of resurrection* that will take place *at the Second Coming of Jesus*.

3. Q. Are you saying that my precious mother is lying cold in the ground right now and is not enjoying heaven with Jesus?

Suggested Response:

The Bible teaches in Romans 8:38–39 that nothing can separate us from God's love. That means God's love surrounds His children while they wait in the sleep of death for the resurrection. Because you trust in God, you can have peace in the knowledge that your mother is wrapped in the unfailing love of God while she sleeps in the grave. Just picture an earthly parent holding their sleeping child in a peaceful, loving embrace. That is what the sleep of death is like for every believing child of God.

Death was never a part of God's original plan. It came about *only* because of humanity's disobedience and sin. Although God hates death, He ordained it to work in our favor. Because the dead are asleep in their graves, they do not see the enormity of human suffering on this earth. They are spared the pain of watching their own loved ones suffer disease, heartbreak, and pain. In the sleep of death there is no sense of the passage of time between death and resurrection. Truly, our incredible God has designed death to be a peaceful, assuring experience for His trusting children.

4. Q. 1 Thessalonians 4:14 says that when Jesus comes, "God will bring with Him those who have fallen asleep in [Jesus]." Doesn't this prove that those people are up in heaven now?

Suggested Response:

First, if you accept what the text actually says, that those who have died are asleep in Jesus, then they are unconscious and unaware of where they are. Consequently, what would be the benefit to them to be in heaven before Jesus comes to earth and awakens them to eternal life?

1 Thessalonians 4:13–18 was written specifically to encourage believers who have lost believing loved ones in death, so they would not "grieve like the rest of men, who have no hope" (v. 13). And what basis did he give them for this hope? He assured them that

their loved ones who "sleep in Jesus" will be resurrected, wakened out of their sleep, and united with them again when Jesus returns.

The phrase in verse 14, "God will bring with Him those who sleep in Jesus," means that as God brought Jesus up from the grave, so God will also, at the Second Coming, bring those who are sleeping in Jesus up from the grave. Thus the New English Bible rightly translates this phrase, "God will bring them to life with Jesus." What a blessed hope!

Session 6—The Second Coming

1. Q. Questions about heaven:

Heaven doesn't seem real to me.

If what I've heard about heaven is true—walking around in white robes, playing harps, etc.—it doesn't sound all that attractive to me. I can't imagine sitting in church every day for eternity.

How does the Bible describe what eternity will be like for those who make it?

Suggested Response:

a. According to the Bible, "heaven" is the place where God dwells (Matthew 6:9). It is not a fixed geographical location, but rather is defined by the presence of God. Wherever God dwells is heaven. The eternal home of the saved will be this earth which, subsequent to Jesus' Second Coming, God Himself will restore to a state of perfection (Matthew 5:5; 2 Peter 3:10–13). The Bible says that once He makes this earth new again, God Himself will move here and live with us! (Revelation 21:3). As incredible as it sounds, once God moves to this earth, heaven will actually be right here on this restored planet.

b. Heaven (the new earth) seemed so real to the believers in the Bible that they considered themselves strangers and pilgrims on this earth, on a journey to their true home, "a heavenly one," which God has prepared for them" (Hebrews 11:13–16).

c. The Bible does not give a detailed description of eternal life in the new earth, but it tells us enough to know that it will be real and wonderful. Note some of the characteristics of the new earth:

1) Complete harmony restored in the animal kingdom—no predation. And all the animals will be tame. (Isaiah 11:6–9)

2) No more physical deformities. (Isaiah 35:1–10)

3) No violence. (Isaiah 60:18–22)

4) Planting, building, continual growth in knowledge and skill. (Isaiah 65:17–25)

5) Grand experiences of worship and celebration. (Isaiah 66:22–23)

6) No more hunger, thirst, or tears of sorrow. (Revelation 7:13–17)

7) No more death, mourning, crying, or pain. (1 Corinthians 15:51–54; Revelation 21:4)

8) Reuniting of loved ones separated by death. (1 Thessalonians 4:16–18)

2. Q. How can you say that Jesus' coming is soon? People have been claiming that for centuries.

Suggested Response:

a. Jesus always wanted His people to believe that He is returning soon. Three times in the last book of the Bible He is quoted saying: "'I am coming soon!'" (Revelation 22:7, 12, 20). He wanted His people to always be ready for Him to return at any moment. Note a couple of His statements to this effect:

1) "'Keep watch because you do not know on what day your Lord will come....So you also must be ready, because the Son of Man will come at an hour when you do not expect him.'" (Matthew 24:42, 44)

2) "'Be careful, or your hearts will be weighed down with dissipation, drunkenness and the anxieties of life, and that day

will close on you unexpectedly like a trap....Be always on the watch and pray that you may be able to escape all that is about to happen, and that you may be able to stand before the Son of Man.'" (Luke 21:34, 36)

It would be unfaithful to the Bible and to Jesus Himself not to convey that His return will be soon.

b. While Jesus said no one knows the day or hour when He will return, He did give us signs whereby we might "'know that it is near, right at the door'" (Matthew 24:33, 36). Note some of the signs we have been given to that effect:

1) Wars would increase. (Matthew 24:6–7)

2) Famines would intensify. (Matthew 24:7)

3) Pestilences (diseases) and earthquakes would increase. (Matthew 24:7)

4) Lawlessness and lovelessness would increase. (Matthew 24:12)

5) There would be great increases in knowledge and travel. (Daniel 12:4)

c. Peter said that those who discount the nearness of Jesus' return because it has been proclaimed for a long time are themselves a sign of the last days: "First of all, you must understand that in the last days scoffers will come, scoffing and following their own evil desires. They will say, 'Where is this ""coming"" he promised? Even since our fathers died, everything goes on as it has since the beginning of creation.'...But do not forget this one thing, dear friends: With the Lord a day is like a thousand years, and a thousand years are like a day. The Lord is not slow in keeping his promise, as some understand slowness. He is patient with you, not wanting anyone to perish, but everyone to come to repentance" (2 Peter 3:3–4, 8–9). You can be thankful that He has delayed His coming this long. He wants you and me to be ready! Do you believe you are ready for His return?

3. Q. How can I be ready for Jesus' return?

Suggested Response:

That's an excellent question. There is probably no more important question in life than that.

The answer is given in part in one of the most well-known texts in the Bible. If you know it, say it with me: "'For God so loved the world that He gave His only begotten Son, that whosoever believeth in Him should not perish but have everlasting life" (John 3:16). Another text says, "Believe in the Lord Jesus, and you will be saved..." (Acts 16:30). Again, "If you confess with your mouth, 'Jesus is Lord,' and believe in your heart that God raised him from the dead, you will be saved" (Romans 10:9).

Confessing "Jesus is Lord" means that we not only believe that He died for us and rose again, but that we choose by His grace to follow and obey Him. James said, "Even the demons believe that—and shudder" (James 2:19). The devils believe that Jesus died and rose again, but they don't obey Him. So, James said, "faith without deeds is dead" (James 2:26). Thus Jesus said, a fool "hears these words of mine and does not put them into practice," while a wise man "hears these words of mine and puts them into practice" (Matthew 7:24, 26).

When Jesus instructed His disciples about preparing for His return, He told them, "'Be always on the watch and pray...'" (Luke 21:35). To be "on the watch" means to take God seriously every day of our lives, in every thought and action. To "pray" means to have a relationship with God, where you allow God to speak to you through the Bible, and you commune with Him in prayer. When you begin to do that, asking Him to help you follow what you discover from the Bible, you are ready for Him to come.

Being ready for Jesus to come is a matter of having a daily experience with God. Our readiness for the Second Coming depends on our relationship with Jesus today.

Session 7—Health

1. Q. Do Seventh-day Adventists believe that people have to live according to their health standards in order to be saved?

Suggested Response:

Suppose your child was on drugs and you were pleading with her to get help. If she were to ask you if she had to get off drugs to be saved, how would you answer her? (Then be quiet and let them answer the question. And let your response be guided by how they answer.)

We would agree. The Bible says: "It is by grace you have been saved, through faith—and this not from yourselves, it is the gift of God, not by works, so that no one can boast" (Ephesians 2:8–9). Getting off drugs is not the way to get saved. Accepting Jesus as the Lord of our lives is the way to get saved. And that is true with regard to any lifestyle issue. I do not practice a healthy lifestyle in order to be saved. I have accepted Jesus as the Lord of my life and am saved by His grace. It is *because* Jesus is the Lord of my life that I want to live the healthiest lifestyle, to honor Him who tells me that my body is a temple for His Spirit to dwell in (1 Corinthians 6:19).

What if your daughter asked you if getting off drugs would help her be a better witness for God?

We would agree. The reason the Bible says, "whether you eat or drink or whatever you do, do it all to the glory of God," is because the way we live either enhances or impedes our ability to relate to God, and enhances or impedes our witness for Jesus (1 Corinthians 10:31). That is why the health principles advocated in the Bible are important to me.

2. Q. Does someone have to become a vegetarian to be a Seventh-day Adventist?

Suggested Response:

No. We do require abstinence from things God forbids such as certain unclean meats and alcohol (Leviticus 11; Proverbs 20:1;

23:29–35). Some Seventh-day Adventists eat meat. Seventh-day Adventists are a global church and diets vary depending on the food available in different areas. Vegetarianism is not a standard of membership or of serving in any office or ministry within the church. However, our church potlucks in North America are vegetarian as we recognize that as the optimal diet as established by God in Eden (Genesis 1:29).

Scientific research also bears out the benefits of a vegetarian diet. In the 25-year study of 35,000 Seventh-day Adventists living in California compared to the general population of that state, it was discovered that 56% of Adventists in that study ate meat, 42% were lacto-ovo vegetarians—ate milk, eggs, cheese, etc. but no meat, and 2% were vegans—ate no meat or animal products. Results revealed that meat-eating Adventists had 64%, lacto-ovo vegetarian Adventists had 40%, and vegan Adventists had only 23% of the heart disease rate of the general population. So while all Adventist groups studied fared better than the general population, those who ate no animal products died at only one third the rate of those who ate meat. While that may not in and of itself get someone to heaven, if the goal of life is to live as long and healthy as possible in order to better bring glory to God in our lives on this earth, then this research certainly bears out the value and significance of the original diet God gave in Eden.

Bear in mind that many people throughout history did not have the availability of the rich abundance and variety of whole grains, fresh fruits and vegetables, nuts, and legumes that our modern North American supermarkets stock today. We probably live as close to the conditions that prevailed in the Garden of Eden as any people have throughout history. This provides us with an opportunity to return to the original diet God gave in Eden.

Furthermore, there is evidence in the Bible that a vegetarian diet may be God's ideal for His people again in the last days. The book of Daniel is comprised of prophecies which reach to the last days and stories that highlight characteristics that will enable God's people to stand victoriously through the last days. The first story in the book focuses on Daniel's commitment to maintain a vegetarian diet even in the court of Babylon, and the blessing God provided as a result (Daniel 1:8–20). The occurrence of this story in this book of prophecies on the last days suggests the value of a vegetarian diet for God's last-day people.

3. Q. There is a story somewhere in the Bible in which God told Peter that he should eat meat that God had formerly classified as unclean. So why do you still observe those Old Testament laws on clean and unclean foods?

Suggested Response:

That story occurs in Acts 10. Peter considered Gentiles spiritually unclean and therefore believed it wrong to associate with them. God wanted to send Peter to instruct Cornelius, a Roman centurion whose heart God had prepared to receive the gospel. To prepare Peter for that visit, God gave Peter a vision of unclean foods and instructed him to eat them. Peter knew that God had not changed His law, so what could this vision mean?

"While Peter was wondering about the meaning of the vision," Cornelius's servants arrived at Peter's home requesting that he come to Cornelius's home to teach him the gospel. As the story of Peter's vision was interpreted by the Spirit, Peter gained an understanding of its meaning: "God has shown me that I should not call any *man* common or unclean" (Acts 10:19–20, 28, 34–35).

Peter's vision in Acts 10 was not about God cleansing unclean food, but about God correcting a mistaken belief concerning "unclean" people, a belief that was preventing the gospel from going to the Gentiles.

See the study notes in the *Andews Study Bible* for an extended explanation.

4. Q. Doesn't the Bible say that when Jesus came He declared all foods clean?

Suggested Response:

The text in question is Mark 7:17–19. Newer translations of the Bible tend to favor a translation similar to this one from the NIV: "'Don't you see that nothing that enters a man from the outside can make him unclean? For it doesn't go into his heart but into his stomach, and then out of his body.' (In saying this, Jesus declared all foods 'clean.')" And it is understandable, based on this translation, why someone would think that Jesus may have rescinded the commandment He gave in the Old Testament against eating unclean animals.

However, the following italicized words are not present in the original Greek manuscripts of Mark 7:19: *"In saying this Jesus declared all foods clean."* In the original manuscripts, that entire English sentence in the NIV comes from the following Greek words with the literal translation written over the top:

"Purifying [cleansing]   all   the   foods"

Καθαρίζων πάντα τὰ βρώματα

The King James and New King James Versions of Mark 7:18–19 follow the original more closely when they translate Jesus' full saying: "Do you not perceive that whatever enters a man from outside cannot defile him, because it does not enter his heart but his stomach, and is eliminated, thus purifying all foods." (The underlined phrase was translated from the four-word Greek phrase above.)

In these verses Jesus is in essence saying: "It is what comes out of a man's heart, his thoughts and actions, which determine his spiritual cleanness or uncleanness. It is not what a person eats that makes him spiritually unclean, for his body will assimilate the nutrients from the food he eats and eliminate the waste, thus cleansing or purifying any impurities on the food that come from unwashed hands." This meaning becomes very clear when the entire passage of Mark 7:1–23 is studied. Jesus was defending His disciples who were being criticized for eating with unwashed hands. (Eating with unwashed hands was a Jewish ceremonial law not found in Scripture but imposed by Jewish tradition. While washing one's hands before eating is a good health habit, Jewish leaders had imposed it as one of many such standards by which they judged a person's level of spirituality.)

5. Q. 1 Timothy 4:1–4 says that every creature is good and not to be refused if it is eaten with thanksgiving. This text rescinds God's previous prohibition of certain foods in Leviticus 11.

Suggested Response:

In this text Paul corrects some false doctrine that was both forbidding people to marry and commanding them "to abstain from foods which God created to be received with thanksgiving..." (v. 3, NKJV).

There was a heresy among some early Christians that taught that the body was evil and the spirit was good, and thus anything that was pleasing to the body, the physical senses, was evil and to be avoided. Hence, the command to avoid marriage (because it involves a pleasurable sexual relationship) and any food that was particularly pleasing to the palate. This heresy was forbidding things that God had ordained for humanity's happiness and good.

The statement in verse 4 (NKJV), "every creature of God is good, and nothing is to be refused if it is received with thanksgiving," is neither advocating promiscuity or the eating of foods that God said should not be eaten (Leviticus 11). There are some kinds of fish that are deadly if eaten, and we would consider it unthinkable to eat another person. This text isn't saying just to thank God for every creature God ever made and eat it. It refers to Christian marriage and to "foods which God created to be received with thanksgiving," which the fanatical heresy Paul was addressing commanded people not to partake of. In this text Paul was saying: Those things which God made for our good and happiness are to be received with thanksgiving and enjoyed.

6. Q. I read somewhere in the Bible that we are supposed to drink wine for health purposes. And doesn't modern research bear out that drinking wine is good for you?

Suggested Response:

In 1 Timothy 5:23 Paul counseled Timothy, "Stop drinking only water, and use a little wine because of your stomach and your frequent illness." The original Greek word for wine and pure grape juice are the same in the Bible—*oinos*. In light of the Bible's previous warnings against alcoholic beverages, it is unlikely that Paul is advising a young elder in the church to be drinking such (Proverbs 20:1; 23:29–35). Grapes contain some of the same medicinal qualities found to be contained in wine.

People in France drink more wine and have less heart disease than people in America. But that's deceiving because people in France also eat only half the number of eggs per person, eat 30% less sugar and syrup, 20% less meat, and 73% more fruits, vegetables, and grains than do Americans.

Because of the negative effects of excessive alcohol consumption on personal health (increased risk of heart disease, high blood pressure, liver disease, cancer, neurological disorders, nutritional deficiencies, etc.) and on society as a whole (accidents, crime, etc.), The World Health Organization, The National Academy of Sciences, and The National Academy of Science Food and Nutrition Board, as well as most professional medical researchers in general, do not recommend the consumption of alcohol as a prescription for health. While some studies indicate that moderate amounts of alcohol may have a protective effect on the heart, there are many other and safer ways to provide such effects. The warnings in the Bible against alcohol and the undisputed social ills contributed to by alcohol make it unsafe in any amount for those who have accepted Jesus as their Lord and want their example to be safe for others to follow.

7. Q. I've tried very hard to quit smoking [or any number of other at-risk behaviors] and just can't. I don't think God will hold that against me.

Suggested Response:

If you were offered a billion dollars to quit smoking for a year, would you do it? Most smokers would, even if they had to lock themselves up in a room and have their food shoved in to them under the door for a year. The issue is motivation more than ability.

Christians have the strongest motivation imaginable because their bodies are the dwelling place of God! (1 Corinthians 6:19–20). And the good news is that help is available. God has promised that there is no temptation that cannot be overcome (1 Corinthians 10:13). It may be hard, but not impossible. "I can do everything through him who gives me strength" (Philippians 4:13). God has a thousand ways to help us. When we rely on Him persistently, He will intervene and come to our aid (1 John 5:14–15). Even if you do not have the desire to quit right now, God will give you both the desire and the ability if you ask Him (Matthew 7:7–8; Philippians 2:13). He has covered all the bases.

And you will have a lot of support. I am praying for you. My church has some helpful brochures and an excellent stop smoking program. I get excited for you just thinking about all the possibilities.

8. Q. Does Jesus still heal today?

Suggested Response:

Yes. But not always according to our desires.

God actually gave us instructions for a simple service specifically designed for healing. It involves prayer and anointing oil administered by an elder of the church (James 5:14–15). Included in the instruction is the assurance: "And the prayer offered in faith will make the sick person well; the Lord will raise him up."

God has assured us that He hears and answers every prayer thus offered for healing. However, the healing that occurs is not always physical. The term for healing used in that text is the Greek word *sozo*, which may also be translated "save" or "salvation." Translators must determine how the word should be translated given the context. So the phrase in James 5:15 which the NIV translates, "will make the sick person *well*," the KJV and NKJV translate, "will *save* the sick." The same word is used in verse 20 to refer to spiritual salvation rather than physical healing.

When we pray for healing, we submit our bodies and spirits to God for whatever healing would be in accordance with His will. Sometimes there is a partial or complete physical healing. Other times not. Jesus Himself prayed to be delivered from having to endure the crucifixion, and we are assured that God heard and answered His prayer (Luke 22:39–44; Hebrews 5:7). But He was not delivered from being crucified. His deliverance came later, at the resurrection. In like manner, we humbly submit our desire and prayer for healing to the will of God. If we aren't healed physically, we are assured that our deliverance will also come at the resurrection. Even when there is not immediate physical healing, we are assured that God will provide spiritual healing through which He prepares us to spend eternity with Him.

9. Q. Isn't meat a lot safer today than in times past? Shouldn't this be taken into consideration in discussions on diet and vegetarianism?

Suggested Response:

It is true that refrigeration systems provide a longer preservation time for many foods, including meat. In some ways, however, it's more unsafe than ever to be eating animal products. Meat processing today, driven by marketing pressures, uses methods that would have been considered unthinkable even a few decades ago.

USA Today's June 10, 2003 cover story was on the possibility of people in the U.S. contracting mad cow disease (bovine spongiform encephalopathy, or BSE) which "has killed at least 150 people worldwide since 1996." The only way cows, which are vegetarians by nature, can become infected with BSE is by humans feeding them "infected animal byproducts." The article revealed the shocking news that "in parts of the country where cattle are raised near poultry production areas, it's not uncommon to feed them poultry litter—basically excreta, bedding, spilled feed and feathers." Since poultry *are* fed animal products, "there is concern that spilled feed as well as partially digested feed might end up back in cattle troughs, resulting in the same potential cycle of infection that caused the British outbreak of mad cow. 'It's gross,' says Caroline Smith DeWaal, food safety director of the Center for Science in the Public Interest. 'Until BSE, this was the hidden issue of what the animals were eating.'"

In most areas of the world where a variety of fruits, grains, vegetables, and legumes are available, the safest diet is still the original diet God gave to Adam and Eve in Eden.

Session 8—The Sanctuary

1. Q. How do Adventists make a connection with Daniel 8:14 and the final judgment?

Suggested Response:

The Old Testament feast that served as the annual Day of Judgment for God's chosen people was the Day of Atonement described in Leviticus 16 and 23:26–32. Leviticus 16:30 says, "On this day atonement will be made for you, to *cleanse* you." Daniel 8:14 prophesies that in 2,300 prophetic days, the sanctuary will be "reconsecrated" (NIV) or "*cleansed*" (KJV, NKJV). When the Hebrew Scriptures were translated into the Greek Bible that was used in the days of Jesus and the disciples, the translators chose the same Greek word for "cleansed" in both Leviticus 16:30 and Daniel 8:14. Linguistically and thematically, the cleansing of the sanctuary prophesied in Daniel 8:14 has parallels with the annual day of judgment God proscribed for His people in Leviticus 16. Since Daniel 8:14 was to be fulfilled at "the time of the end" (8:17, 26), it must refer to the temple in heaven (Hebrews 8:1–2), because the temple on earth was destroyed permanently in 70 A.D. by the Romans. This suggests that Daniel 8:14 refers to a phase of God's judgment that is to take place in heaven at a specific time in history—at the end of the 2,300 prophetic days. Jesus said that when He returns He will bring everyone's reward with Him (Matthew 16:27; Revelation 22:12). So the phase of the final judgment that determines rewards has already been completed by then. That's the pre-advent or investigative phase of the judgment that was prophesied in Daniel 8:14. It's described in Daniel 7:9–14 as taking place in the presence of heavenly beings (vv. 9–10) before Jesus comes (vv. 13–14).

2. Q. How do Adventists get 1844 out of Daniel 8:14?

Suggested Response:

Daniel 8:14 prophesies that the sanctuary in heaven will be cleansed after "2,300 evenings and mornings" (NIV), "two thousand three hundred days" (KJV, NKJV). When the Bible refers to "days" in prophecy, it signifies years (Numbers 14:34; Ezekiel 4:6). The angel explicitly informed Daniel that this long time prophecy of 2,300 years "concerns the distant future" and reaches to "the time of the end" (Daniel 8:17, 26). Daniel himself did not understand the meaning of this prophecy, for it reached far beyond his day. He said, "I was appalled by the vision; it was beyond understanding" (8:27). About twelve years later an angel visited Daniel and proclaimed: "I have now come to give you insight and understanding....Therefore, consider the message and understand the vision" (9:21, 23). The angel then gave Daniel another prophecy that coincided with the beginning of the 2,300-year prophecy, both of which began with "the decree to restore and rebuild Jerusalem" (9:25). The final issuance of the decree to restore Jerusalem occurred "in the seventh year of Artaxerxes," king of Persia, or 457 B.C. Twenty-three hundred years later stretches to 1844. Thus the 2,300 prophetic days of Daniel 8:14 reached from 457 B.C. to 1844 A.D.

3. Q. Early Adventists were naïve, religious fanatics who taught that the world would end in 1844. Doesn't it bother you that the Adventist church began with such an embarrassing prophetic miscalculation?

Suggested Response:

A few of the pioneers of the Seventh-day Adventist Church had indeed been part of the Millerite movement who believed that the world would end in 1844, based on the misunderstanding that the reference to "the sanctuary" in Daniel 8:14 referred to this world. But the Millerite movement was not made up of Seventh-day Adventists. The Seventh-day Adventist Church was not officially organized for another 20 years. The vast majority of Millerites splintered into numerous factions, returned to their former churches, or became unbelievers. Those few who were part of the Millerite movement and later became pioneers of the Seventh-day Adventist Church used their bitter experience and great disappointment in 1844 as a catalyst to restudy the Scriptures to gain a clearer understanding of the prophecies and the gospel. It was that continuing, intense study of the Scriptures, not the faulty understanding of prophecy held by the Millerites, that ultimately led those earnest Bible students from a variety of Protestant denominations to form the Seventh-day Adventist church.

4. Q. Do you Adventists believe that God was the one who misled the Millerites into thinking that the end of the world would occur in 1844?

Suggested Response:

For 40-plus years between the time when God delivered Israel out of slavery in Egypt and the time He led them into the Promised Land, He led them everywhere they went by a pillar of cloud and fire (Exodus 13:20–22; 40:34–38). God led them into places where there was no water, no food, no natural way of escape at the Red Sea, etc. (Exodus 14:10–20; 17:1–7; Psalm 78:12–16; etc.). By leading them into places of trial and temptation, He tested them, seeking to mature their faith and groom them into a mighty missionary movement. While God doesn't directly lead people into error, He motivates them to study His word, even if He knows they may not come to a perfect understanding on every point. Those few Millerites who were to later become pioneers of the Seventh-day Adventist faith saw their sweet/bitter experience in 1844 mirrored in the Revelation 10:8–10 prophecy of eating a little book (Daniel) which would be sweet in the mouth but bitter in the belly. And in that same chapter of Revelation they gained two more insights of extreme importance. First, the angel of Revelation 10 who gave the command to eat the little book and described the sweet/bitter results it would have, was "robed in a cloud...and his legs were fiery pillars," which assured them that God had been with them, even leading them, through their bitter 1844 experience, even as He had led His people of old by the pillar of cloud and fire (10:1). And second, they discovered their mission in the words of the angel: "You must prophesy again about many peoples, nations, languages and kings" (10:11). God had certainly accompanied, if not directly led, a group of earnest Bible students through an extremely trying spiritual and emotional experience that ultimately gave birth to the worldwide Seventh-day Adventist missionary movement.

Session 9—The Seventh-day Adventist Movement

Q. What is Ellen G. White's role, relative to the Bible, in the Seventh-day Adventist Church?

Possible Answer: Seventh-day Adventists believe that in the ministry and writings of Ellen G. White, God manifested the prophetic gift similarly to how He manifested it through the Bible prophets of old. However, "We do not believe that the writings of Ellen White are an addition to the canon of Scripture...[or] function as the foundation and final authority of Christian faith as does Scripture...[or] may be used as the basis of doctrine...[or] are essential for the proclamation of the truths of Scripture to society at large." We also "do not believe that Scripture can be understood only through the writings of Ellen White...[or] "that the writings of Ellen White exhaust the meaning of Scripture."[6]

Ellen White herself pointed to the Bible as the foundation for Seventh-day Adventist faith and practice, and as such she expected

---

6. "The Inspiration and Authority of the Ellen G. White Writings," Seventh-day Adventist Biblical Research Institute, *Ministry*, February 1983, p. 24.

that her writings would be judged by the teaching of Scripture, not Scripture by her writings. She referred to her ministry as a "lesser light to lead men and women to the greater light."[7]

We believe, therefore, that "a correct understanding of the inspiration and authority of the writings of Ellen White will avoid two extremes: (1) regarding these writings as functioning on a canonical level identical with Scripture, or (2) considering them as ordinary Christian literature."[8]

In the Statement of Fundamental Beliefs voted by the General Conference of Seventh-day Adventists at Dallas in April, 1980, the Preamble states: "Seventh-day Adventists accept the Bible as their only creed and hold certain fundamental beliefs to be the teaching of the Holy Scriptures." Paragraph one reflects the church's understanding of the inspiration and authority of the Scriptures, while paragraph seventeen reflects the church's understanding of the inspiration and authority of the writings of Ellen White in relation to the Scriptures. These paragraphs read as follows:

1. The Holy Scriptures

"The Holy Scriptures, Old and New Testaments, are the written Word of God, given by divine inspiration through holy men of God who spoke and wrote as they were moved by the Holy Spirit. In this Word, God has committed to man the knowledge necessary for salvation. The Holy Scriptures are the infallible revelation of His will. They are the standard of character, the test of experience, the authoritative revealer of doctrines, and the trustworthy record of God's acts in history. (2 Peter 1:20, 21; 2 Tim. 3:16, 17; Ps. 119:105; Prov. 30:5, 6; Isa. 8:20; John 17:17; 1 Thess. 2:13; Heb. 4:12.)"

17. The Gift of Prophecy

"One of the gifts of the Holy Spirit is prophecy. This gift is an identifying mark of the remnant church and was manifested in the ministry of Ellen G. White. As the Lord's messenger, her writings are a continuing and authoritative source of truth which provide

---

7. Ellen G. White, *Colporteur Ministry*, 125.
8. "The Inspiration and Authority of the Ellen G. White Writings," p. 24.

for the church comfort, guidance, instruction, and correction. They also make clear that the Bible is the standard by which all teaching and experience must be tested. (Joel 2:28, 29; Acts 2:14-21; Heb. 1:1-3; Rev. 12:17; 19:10.)"

The following affirmations and denials speak to the issues which have been raised about the inspiration and authority of the Ellen White writings and their relation to the Bible. These clarifications should be taken as a whole. They are an attempt to express the present understanding of Seventh-day Adventists. They are not to be construed as a substitute for, or a part of, the two doctrinal statements quoted above.

"The Seventh-day Adventist Church's Understanding of Ellen White's Authority"

AFFIRMATIONS

1. We believe that Scripture is the divinely revealed Word of God and is inspired by the Holy Spirit.

2. We believe that the canon of Scripture is composed only of the sixty-six books of the Old and New Testaments.

3. We believe that Scripture is the foundation of faith and the final authority in all matters of doctrine and practice.

4. We believe that Scripture is the Word of God in human language.

5. We believe that Scripture teaches that the gift of prophecy will be manifest in the Christian church after New Testament times.

6. We believe that the ministry and writings of Ellen White were a manifestation of the gift of prophecy.

7. We believe that Ellen White was inspired by the Holy Spirit and that her writings, the product of that inspiration, are applicable and authoritative, especially to Seventh-day Adventists.

8. We believe that the purposes of the Ellen White writings include guidance in understanding the teaching of Scripture and application of these teachings, with prophetic urgency, to the spiritual and moral life.

9. We believe that the acceptance of the prophetic gift of Ellen White is important to the nurture and unity of the Seventh-day Adventist Church.

10. We believe that Ellen White's use of literary sources and assistants finds parallels in some of the writings of the Bible.

DENIALS

1. We do not believe that the quality or degree of inspiration in the writings of Ellen White is different from that of Scripture.

2. We do not believe that the writings of Ellen White are an addition to the canon of Sacred Scripture.

3. We do not believe that the writings of Ellen White function as the foundation and final authority of Christian faith as does Scripture.

4. We do not believe that the writings of Ellen White may be used as the basis of doctrine.

5. We do not believe that the study of the writings of Ellen White may be used to replace the study of Scripture.

6. We do not believe that Scripture can be understood only through the writings of Ellen White.

7. We do not believe that the writings of Ellen White exhaust the meaning of Scripture.

8. We do not believe that the writings of Ellen White are essential for the proclamation of the truths of Scripture to society at large.

9. We do not believe that the writings of Ellen White are the product of mere Christian piety.

10. We do not believe that Ellen White's use of literary sources and assistants negates the inspiration of her writings.

Read Ellen White [9]

Roger L. Dudley, Ed.D., and Des Cummings, Jr., Phd.
Institute of Church Ministry, Andrews University

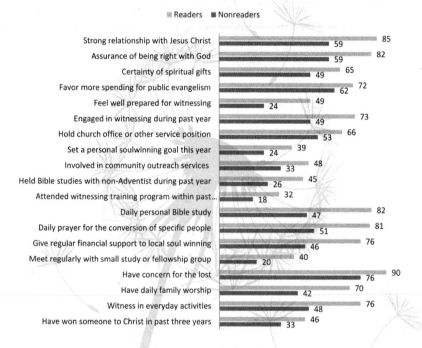

Readers ▪ Nonreaders

	Readers	Nonreaders
Strong relationship with Jesus Christ	59	85
Assurance of being right with God	59	82
Certainty of spiritual gifts	49	65
Favor more spending for public evangelism	62	72
Feel well prepared for witnessing	24	49
Engaged in witnessing during past year	49	73
Hold church office or other service position	53	66
Set a personal soulwinning goal this year	24	39
Involved in community outreach services	33	48
Held Bible studies with non-Adventist during past year	26	45
Attended witnessing training program within past...	18	32
Daily personal Bible study	47	82
Daily prayer for the conversion of specific people	51	81
Give regular financial support to local soul winning	46	76
Meet regularly with small study or fellowship group	20	40
Have concern for the lost	76	90
Have daily family worship	42	70
Witness in everyday activities	48	76
Have won someone to Christ in past three years	33	46

---

9. Roger L. Dudley, Des Cummings, Jr., "Who Reads Ellen White?" *Ministry*, October, 1982, pp. 10–12. These researchers add: "Seldom does a research study find the evidence so heavily weighted toward one conclusion. In the church growth survey, on *every single item* that deals with personal attitudes or practices, the member who regularly studies Ellen White's books tends to rate higher than does the member who reads them occasionally or never....On no item do nonreaders rate higher than readers." (Emphasis in original.)

APPENDIX B

Pray for those on your impact list:

That God will draw them to Himself (John 6:44)

That they seek to know God (Acts 17:27)

That they believe the Word of God (1 Thessalonians 2:13)

That Satan is bound from blinding them to the truth and that his influences in their life be "cast down" (2 Corinthians 4:4; 10:4–5)

That the Holy Spirit works in them (John 16:8–13)

That they turn from sin (Acts 3:19)

That they believe in Christ as Savior (John 1:12)

That they obey Christ as Lord (Matthew 7:21)

That they take root and grow in Christ (Colossians 2:6–7)

These are taken from *The Praying Church Source Book* by Alvin J. Vander Griend and Edith Bajema (2nd ed.; Grand Rapids, Michigan: Faith Alive Christian Resources, 1997), pages 128–129.

APPENDIX C

RECOMMENDED RESOURCES

GENERAL TOPICS

Andrews Study Bible

The Andrews Study Bible is an innovative and practical presentation of the Scriptures designed for both the new believer and the experienced Bible student. It is the only formal, full-featured study Bible ever published by a Seventh-day Adventist publishing house. It was sponsored by the General Conference, through Andrews University. It contains more than 12,000 page-by-page study notes written by faithful Adventist teachers from around the world, and contains a unique, linked reference system to highlight the great themes of the Christian faith as understood by Seventh-day Adventists. It is the most comprehensive Bible available to study Adventist teachings in a thorough and systematic way, and is thus ideal for personal witnessing. It is the ideal Bible to give to others to introduce them to the great teachings of the Bible as highlighted in the Contagious Adventist seminar.

Website: www.universitypress.andrews.edu
Phone number: 269-471-6134 or 1-800-467-6369
Email address: aupo@andrews.edu

Questions on Doctrine: Annotated Edition
Notes with historical and theological introduction by George R. Knight

This volume is a completely new typeset of the monumental 1957 classic. It is the best work available by the church to address typical questions about the major teachings of Scripture as understood by Seventh-day Adventists. Thus, it is of great value to help the Contagious Adventist prepare to answer the challenges to key Bible teachings that Adventists uphold and proclaim. No Contagious Adventist library is complete without this important resource.

Website: www.universitypress.andrews.edu
Phone number: 269-471-6134 or 1-800-467-6369
Email address: aupo@andrews.edu

Light Link, Bible Chain Reference System

A unique chain reference system on pre-cut decals that covers the twenty-eight Bible doctrines of Adventism. There are ten texts for each of the twenty-eight Bible teachings, with the clearest most persuasive texts listed first. Each Bible marking kit comes with clear installation instructions and everything needed to quickly upgrade your Bible to a new level of usefulness. Light Link is carefully designed to work well with any translation of the Bible and the decals are easily installed in a new or favorite Bible.

How to Order: Light Link is carried in most Adventist Book Stores. You can order it on-line with PayPal at www.yourlightlink.com or place an order by phone at (269) 471-6143.

SESSION TOPICS

1. Why Become a Contagious Adventist

Christian Service, Ellen White
This call to consecrated service in the science of soul winning will be invaluable to ministers, teachers, church leaders, and others interested in soul winning.

2. Jesus Is Lord

Steps to Christ, Ellen White
One of the great spiritual classics of all time, this book is a meaningful guide to Christian living.

3. The Great Controversy

The Great Controversy, Ellen White
The Great Controversy gives a startling overview of the mighty conflict between Christ and Satan from its origins in heaven thousands of years ago to its conclusion on earth in the days just ahead of us. This

still-timely book reveals how God will ultimately rid the universe of evil and make all things new. The author powerfully points out the principles involved in the impending conflict and how each person can stand firmly for God and His truth.

4. The Sabbath

A Bridge Across Time, Dan M. Appel

This warm, friendly book weaves biblical reasons for Sabbath-keeping into a plot based on a boss-employee friendship.

Website: www.adventistbookcenter.com

The Lost Meaning of the Seventh Day, Sigve K. Tonstad

Sigve K. Tonstad recovers the profound and foundational understanding of God that can be experienced in the seventh day, showing that Scripture has consistently asserted that the Sabbath of Creation is the Sabbath of the whole story of how God makes right what has gone wrong in the world. This sweeping work of biblical theology and historical analysis traces the seventh day as it is woven throughout Scripture and the history of Christianity.

Website: www.universitypress.andrews.edu
Phone number: 269-471-6134 or 1-800-467-6369
Email address: aupo@andrews.edu

In Granite or Ingrained? What the Old and New Covenants Reveal about the Gospel, the Law, and the Sabbath, Skip MacCarty

Contagious Adventists will frequently be challenged that God's law, and particularly the Sabbath, are no longer relevant because we live in the era of the "new covenant." These popular claims about the old and new covenants have diminished the gospel and narrowed the faith and spiritual life of millions of Christians. In this book and its study guide, Contagious Adventists have a great resource that demonstrates the dynamic element of the gospel in the profound relationship between love and law. They will better understand the apparent dichotomy of old and new covenants in the New Testament, and be better equipped to share why the perpetuity of the Sabbath is fully affirmed throughout Scripture.

Website: www.universitypress.andrews.edu
Phone number: 269-471-6134 or 1-800-467-6369
Email address: aupo@andrews.edu

Why I Go to Church on Sunday, David Merling, Sr.
This little booklet surveys ten reasons people give for why they go to church on Sunday. Then the author helps us address these reasons.

To order: Contact David Merling
2009 Twisted Juniper Road • Rio Rancho, New Mexico 87124
Home: (505) 792–2626 • Cell: (505) 217–4747
Email address: davidmerling@gmail.com

5. Death and Beyond

The Rich Man and Lazarus, Dennis Crews
By comparing Scripture with Scripture this booklet helps us understand what Jesus meant in the Luke 16:19–31 parable about the Rich Man and Lazarus.

To order call the ABC: 877-227-4800 or visit the Amazing Facts website and get a free downloadable PDF of the complete booklet.

6. The Second Coming

What Left Behind Left Behind, Dwight K. Nelson
This book deals with the second coming, secret rapture theory, and dispensationalism. Published by the Review & Herald Publishing Association.

7. Health

Balance Magazine and Lifestyle Matters Seminar Kits. Call LifestyleMatters TM to order some attractive "Balance" magazines to put on your desk at work or share with your friends. These are great conversation starters. Visit their website to view the material: www.lifestylematters.com Click SHOP; click *Balance* Magazine. Call: 866–624–5433 to order.

8. The Sanctuary

DVD *The Midnight Cry! William Miller & the End of the World*

In the face of much opposition, hundreds of thousands of Americans believed or hoped or perhaps feared that the world would be destroyed by fire at the Second Coming of Christ on October 22, 1844. This feature-length film documentary, narrated by Academy Award-winning actor Cliff Robertson, tells this poignant story of one of the most remarkable episodes in the history of modern religion when citizens urged a nation to prepare to meet their God. It provides the best audio-visual presentation available about the historical rise of Adventism, and helps viewers understand better why a movement can, today, be fully committed to the on-going relevance of the great prophecies of the book of Daniel.

Website: www.universitypress.andrews.edu

Phone number: 269-471-6134 or 1-800-467-6369

Email address: aupo@andrews.edu

1844 Made Simple, Clifford Goldstein

What significance, if any, does the year 1844 and the oft attacked events surrounding it have for Christians today? Is there a way to make sense of the confusing maze of beasts, dates, and kingdoms in Daniel?

Website: www.adventistbookcenter.com

Graffiti in the Holy of Holies, Clifford Goldstein

Current attacks on the sanctuary and Ellen White take aim at the heart of Adventism. Clifford Goldstein responds in *Graffiti in the Holy of Holies.* Arguably his most important book in a decade, this book dissects the arguments being leveled at the investigative judgment and the Spirit of Prophecy revealing solid ground for our faith in both.

Website: www.adventistbookcenter.com

Who's Afraid of the Judgment?, Roy Gane

The judgment. Most Christians do not understand it. Others ignore it or cringe in terror because of it.

Website: www.adventistbookcenter.com

Christ In His Sanctuary, Ellen White

An important work by Ellen White back in print. This book includes valuable information on investigative judgment and will appeal to those interested in the heavenly sanctuary and Jesus' ministry in the inner compartment. A valuable asset to any Adventist library.

Website: www.adventistbookcenter.com

9. The Seventh-day Adventist Movement

DVD La Ventana—"The Window"

This DVD portrays the dramatized story of a couple who reaches their neighbors for Christ through the simple power of friendship (30 minutes). It shows members how they too can win their neighbors through prayer, friendship, and meeting practical needs. The original video was produced in Spanish (with English subtitles), but it now has been dubbed into English to make it user friendly to Anglo audiences.

To order: Contact Jorge Mayer
Cell: 404-432-9098
Email address: jmayer@southernunion.com

The Chosen, Dwight K. Nelson

This 366-page devotional book deals with Adventist spirituality and every major Bible teaching we have raised up to share with the world. There is a major segment which addresses the concepts of witnessing and personal testimony.